Great
Stanley Cup
Playoffs

*Exciting accounts of classic battles to determine
the winner of hockey's symbol of supremacy—the
Stanley Cup.*

Great Stanley Cup Playoffs

by Bill Libby

Illustrated with photographs

Random House
New York

PRO HOCKEY
LIBRARY

To the best hockey fans I've known, Sy "Lefty"
Adelson, who taught me much about the game,
and to Paul "Iron Man" Gardella, whose streak of
consecutive Ranger games observed, dissected and
criticized has gone well past ten seasons. Also to
Mickey and Eddie and others of the old faithful
Garden group.

PICTURE CREDITS: Canada Wide-Pictorial Parade, 12, 58–59, 117, 126–127,
138–139; H. W. Tetlow-Pictorial Parade, 67, 114; United Press International,
endpapers, 3, 6, 19, 22–23, 26, 31, 32–33, 35, 38, 48, 53, 54–55, 62, 64 (top right),
70 (top), 75, 81, 86, 89, 90–91, 95, 96–97, 100–101, 103, 106, 110, 118–119, 130,
134, 142, 145 (top), 147; Wide World Photos, 15, 44, 51, 64 (top left, bottom), 70
(bottom), 78, 80, 122, 145 (bottom).

Cover photo: Ken Regan—Camera 5

Library of Congress Cataloging in Publication Data
Libby, Bill.
Great Stanley Cup playoffs.
(Pro-hockey library, #4)
SUMMARY: A brief history of the Stanley Cup accompanies accounts
of the stars and events of some of the most outstanding playoffs.
1. Stanley Cup (Hockey)—Juvenile literature.
[1. Stanley Cup (Hockey) 2. Hockey] I. Title.
GV847.7.L5   796.9'62   72-1593
ISBN 0-394-82404-0   ISBN 0-394-92404-5 (lib. bdg.)

Contents

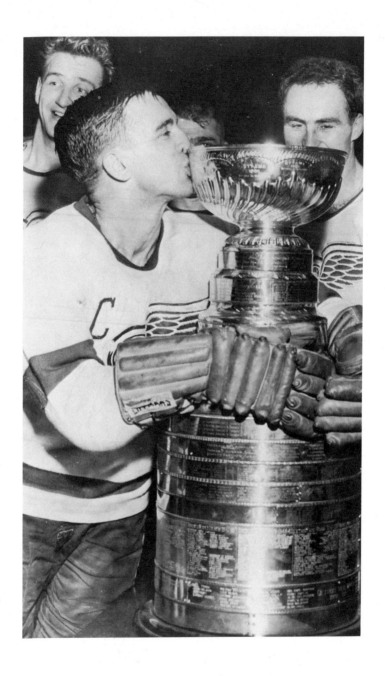

Introduction

The origins of ice hockey are lost in antiquity. There is evidence that field hockey was played 2,500 years ago in Greece. Centuries later, in a colder climate, a similar game was played on ice by men on skates. A rough form of ice hockey as we now know it was played in Europe and North America in the early 1800s. Then formal rules were drawn up in Canada in the 1870s and leagues for team play were formed in the 1880s. Soon ice hockey was Canada's national sport. It now is played in many countries and is a regular event in the winter Olympics. But Canada remains the true home of the sport. Today most teams in the National Hockey League are based in the United States, but almost all NHL players still come from Canada.

Early in the 1890s, an Englishman, Frederick Arthur, Lord Stanley of Preston, who was then Governor General of Canada, became enthusiastic about ice hockey. He directed the construction of an outdoor rink and the formation of a "government team." Then in 1892 he donated a trophy to be given each year to the leading team in Canada. He paid ten pounds—$48.67 in U.S. money at the time —for the purchase of a gold-lined silver bowl mounted on an ebony base. This bowl soon was known as the Stanley Cup. Men since have shed blood and gone broke trying to capture it.

In the 1890s hockey was an amateur sport and there was little formal organization. To determine the first holder of the Cup, a single game playoff was staged in 1893 between the Montreal Amateur Athletic Association team and the Osgoode Hall team of Ottawa. Montreal won and gained the silverware. Lord Stanley already had returned to London. He never saw a Stanley Cup game.

In time, tournaments were staged to determine the yearly winner. Some teams traveled from the far corners of the country to try for it. As hockey's popularity grew, teams began to pay prized players to gain their services. In 1910 the professional National Hockey Association (NHA) was formed and it was decided that the Stanley Cup should go annually to the NHA champion. A few years later a strong Pacific Coast League was formed and the Cup winner was determined in a playoff between the Pacific Coast League champion and the NHA champion. In 1917 the National Hockey League (NHL) replaced the NHA. Until 1927 the Stanley Cup was still given to the winner of the Pacific Coast–NHL playoff. Then the PCL dropped out of competition and the Cup became the symbol of the NHL championship.

Over the years, the Cup itself changed in appearance. A new 3-foot-high base is made of panels on which the names of the players of each winning team are engraved. It is the fondest ambition of most players to have their names appear there. Although some have their names on the trophy more than once, most hockey players never get their names on it.

The number of teams in the National Hockey League has changed many times over the years. But six have been in the league for forty years or more— the Montreal Canadiens, Toronto Maple Leafs, Detroit Red Wings, Chicago Black Hawks, Boston Bruins and New York Rangers. From the early 1940s through the 1966–67 season, these six teams made up the NHL all by themselves.

The league doubled in size in the 1967–68 season with the addition of six more teams—the St. Louis Blues, Philadelphia Flyers, Minnesota North Stars, Los Angeles Kings, Pittsburgh Penguins and Oakland Seals. Three years later the Vancouver Canucks and Buffalo Sabres were admitted. Then in 1972–73 teams in Atlanta and Long Island (New York) brought the NHL total to 16 teams.

There are other trophies to be won in the NHL. The winner of the East Division regular-season championship takes possession of the Prince of Wales Trophy, and the West Division champ gets the Clarence Campbell Bowl. But the first job of any NHL team is to qualify for the Stanley Cup playoffs, which begin at the end of regular-season play. In the old six-team league, four of the six teams qualified for the playoffs. In the expanded NHL eight teams qualify. Teams work hard to avoid elimination from the post-season play and to gain the best positions for the playoffs. They can finish far behind the first-place team, losing more games than they win, but if they make the playoffs, their season is considered a success. And some such teams have gone on to capture the Cup.

The Montreal Canadiens have held the Cup most often, winning it 16 times, including wins in 1968, 1969 and 1971. They also set a record by holding the Cup for five straight years, winning the playoffs each year from 1956 through 1960. Toronto also had spectacular playoff ability. Although they had won regular-season championships only twice, they won the Stanley Cup ten times, including two strings of three in a row. Detroit had seven championships.

Aside from the expansion teams, which had never won the Cup, the New York Rangers have won it the fewest times, only twice. The Chicago Black Hawks captured it three times.

In 1970 the Boston Bruins, boasting two of hockey's greatest stars, Bobby Orr and Phil Esposito, took aim at their fourth Stanley Cup. The story of the 1970 Bruins makes a good starting place for *Great Stanley Cup Playoffs*.

1. The Big, Bad Bruins

Bobby Orr was greeted as a hero who would take his team to the championship even before he played a major league game. Slim, stylish and explosive, he was regarded as the most brilliant prospect in the history of hockey. According to the rules then in effect, an NHL team could claim a player when he was 14 years old. The Boston Bruins signed Orr on his 14th birthday, supervised his development and waited eagerly for him to turn 18 when he would be eligible for professional play. Bruin fans were promised that Bobby would bring the team up from the bottom of the league where it had rested for so many seasons.

Orr was a defenseman but he played like a forward. He was an especially swift and agile skater and he seemed able to do tricks with the puck. Stealing the puck from the opposition, he would rush from his defense position toward the goal. He could shoot or pass spectacularly and his aggressiveness inspired his team and demoralized the opposition. No youngster in sports history ever was more eagerly awaited by his team.

Bobby Orr.

The Bruins had not finished first in regular-season play or captured the Stanley Cup since 1941. Then Orr was rushed right into a Bruin uniform for the 1966–67 season and Boston fans expected a miracle. Much to their disappointment, the Bruins remained at the bottom, finishing last and missing the playoffs for the eighth straight season.

The season was a rough one for Bobby. The tough men in this tough sport tested him, checking him relentlessly, hitting him hard, picking fights with him. They found out he was tough, too. Hockey is played with sticks and sharp skates and flying fists, and injuries are common. But according to NHL tradition, the good players get quick first aid and return to action. Orr did that and he gave as much as he got on the ice. But he injured a knee which slowed him up and he found that NHL hockey was a big adjustment for an 18-year-old rookie.

After one game that rookie year he sighed and said, "The pressure is pretty heavy. Everyone expects an awful lot from me. I'm trying to produce, but the other guys are all over me. They're good, the greatest. I find it a little hard to believe I'm supposed to beat them. They're giving it to me pretty good. I won't back down. But it's getting to me some."

His face was flushed and sweat streamed from his sandy hair. He was bleeding from a nick alongside one eye. His arms and legs were bruised. He looked very young and thin and tired. He said, "I'll be all right. It'll just take some time. They have to give me some time."

It did not take long. By the next season, 1967–68, Orr's Bruins had risen to third place and into the playoffs. But they lost in the first round. And in 1968–69 they had finished second, only three points behind mighty Montreal. They faced the Canadiens in the semi-finals of the playoffs, losing in six games. Three of Montreal's four victories were in overtime and the fourth win was in double-overtime.

The Bruins still lacked the Cup, but Bobby was the talk of the hockey world. He had revolutionized defensive play. If not the best defensive defenseman in the game, he had proven he could cover up with enormous effectiveness while taking off on rushes to the goal. Every young defenseman in the sport was watching and beginning to think of carrying the puck and scoring goals, as well as standing back and giving body-checks.

The Bruin team was beginning to jell. General manager Milt Schmidt, a Bruin hero of earlier days, signed a young, ambitious and imaginative coach, Harry Sinden. Phil Esposito, Ken Hodge and Fred Stanfield came from Chicago in a trade. With captain Johnny Bucyk, they provided punch in the front line. In addition there were tough veterans like John McKenzie and Teddy Green and young Derek Sanderson, a mod young man with long hair and fancy clothes. Gerry Cheevers and Ed Johnston got the job done in the nets. Sinden's style was to play it tough and Boston brawled along, becoming known as "The Big, Bad Bruins." The Bruins outscored their foes consistently.

Big Phil Esposito, an enormously talented center, had played in the shadow of Bobby Hull at Chicago. But in Boston he began to shine. In 1969 Espo had scored 49 goals and led the league with 77 assists and 126 points. Some fans began to think that he was as brilliant as Hull. That same year Orr had scored 21 goals and assisted on more than twice that many.

In 1969–70 the Bruins were ready. Orr set new all-time records for defensemen. He scored 33 goals and led the league with 87 assists for a total of 120 points. He was the first defenseman ever to lead the league in scoring points. Espo added 43 goals and totaled 99 points. The Bruins had suffered a setback before the season when Teddy Green was critically injured in a stick-fight. Even so, the brawling Bostonians tied with Chicago for first in the East Division.

Chicago won 45 games, lost 22 and tied 9. Boston won 40 games, lost 17 and tied 19. With two points for each victory and one for each tie, each team had 99. Chicago was awarded the pennant and the Prince of Wales Trophy because they had more victories, even though the Bruins had fewer defeats. But both teams were more concerned with another trophy, the Stanley Cup. Boston had not won the Cup in 29 years.

For the first time in NHL history, no Canadian team had made the playoffs. New York, which led the league for 16 weeks before falling into a slump, had finished in a fourth-place tie with Montreal. The Rangers gained the playoff berth in the East because they had scored two more goals than the Canadiens. So in the opening round Boston would play New York, while Chicago opposed Detroit. Over in the West Division the expansion teams played against each other. St. Louis had won the pennant in the West with a poorer record than Montreal's. The Blues took on Minnesota, while Pittsburgh tackled Oakland.

In the opening game against New York, Esposito scored three goals for a hat trick and the Bruins routed the Rangers 8-2. Ranger coach Emile Francis relieved regular goalie Ed Giacomin in the second game, turning instead to 40-year-old Terry Sawchuk. The Rangers battled back, but the Bruins rallied for a 5-3 triumph. The lusty Boston fans cheered their team on.

The series then moved to New York. Francis used Giacomin in goal and the Rangers rewarded their supporters with back-to-back victories to even the series at two victories apiece.

Back in Boston Garden for the fifth game, Orr got

Phil Esposito scores for the Bruins.

the Bruins off to an early lead. Then the Rangers rallied and went ahead 2-1. But Esposito knocked in goals midway in the second period and early in the third for a 3-2 triumph. In the sixth game Orr scored twice and the Bruins romped home, winning 4-1, and taking the series four victories to two. Meanwhile, Chicago beat Detroit in six games.

So the Bruins would face Chicago in the semi-finals. In a way, the Boston-Chicago series was a playoff for first place in the East as well as a Stanley Cup playoff. In addition, Phil Esposito would be opposing his younger brother Tony, the brilliant rookie Chicago netminder who had recorded a record 15 shutouts during the regular season. "When it comes to getting goals and winning games, I'd try to beat my own mother," smiled Phil.

The first two games were played in Chicago's cavernous stadium. In game one, Bobby Hull and stylish Stan Mikita started off quickly for the Hawks. Hawk defenseman Keith Magnuson played well in front of goaler Esposito. But the Bruins were blazing. Boston's Esposito beat his brother after 12 minutes of the first period, then again four minutes later. Late in the third period Phil scored again, chalking up the hat trick against Tony. On defense, Bruin Ed Westfall shadowed Hull and shut him out. The Bruins won 6-3. In the second game, Orr started the scoring and Esposito finished it. The Hawks fell again, 4-1, and Hull was shut out again.

Losing the two first games at home seemed to discourage the Hawks. In Boston for the third game they were burned, 5-2. Espo scored and Hull did not.

The Hawks were in danger of losing four straight. In the fourth game Hull shifted from left wing to center in an effort to escape Westfall's defense, but Westfall stayed with him. Bruins Don Marcotte and Bucyk blasted in first-period goals to give Boston a 2-0 lead.

Then in the second period Magnuson scored for the Hawks and Dennis Hull, Bobby's brother, tallied twice to put the Hawks ahead 3-2. But the Bruins' Fred Stanfield scored to tie it up again. The fans in the Boston Garden were wild with excitement. But on the ice the going was hard.

In the fifth minute of the third period Bryan Campbell put the Hawks ahead again, 4-3, and the Chicagoans struggled to protect their lead. But with less than five minutes left, Ken Hodge of the Bruins got his stick on the puck in front of the Hawk nets and drove it past Tony Esposito to tie the game. The fans came to their feet roaring. When the struggle resumed, it seemed certain the two teams would head into overtime. First Tony Esposito, then Boston goalie Cheevers, dove to make remarkable saves in the nets. But then, suddenly, with less than two minutes to play, the Bruins' tough, stocky John McKenzie batted the black disc beyond Esposito's reach, the red light blazed again and Boston led, 5-4.

In the last seconds Bobby Hull led several Black Hawk drives on the goal. But the siren finally sounded and it was all over. Hull had been shut out and the Bruins had swept the series.

Now it was on to the finals, against St. Louis, which had beaten Minnesota and struggled seven games to turn back Pittsburgh. Now, it was thought,

Chicago goalie Tony Esposito (Phil's brother) shows his dejection after the Bruins' John MacKenzie scores the winning goal.

Boston could coast to the Stanley Cup. The Blues, only in their third year in the NHL, were no match for the Black Hawks or the Bruins, observers said. However, even an expansion club like St. Louis could draw inspiration from nearness to Lord Stanley's silverware. They had a fierce, resourceful coach in Scotty Bowman, a strong scorer and leader in Red Berenson and three able goalies—the aging but brilliant Glenn Hall, veteran Jacques Plante and the young and promising Ernie Wakely.

The first two games were played on the Blues' home ice. But even this advantage was not enough. Bucyk blasted in three goals and Esposito one to lead a 6-1 romp in the opener. Derek Sanderson scored a pair in the second game to pace a 6-2 Bruin victory. On almost every score, Esposito and Orr seemed to be assisting. They were all over the ice.

Back in Boston, Bruin fans were hungry. If the Bruins could win two games, they would win without having to go back to St. Louis. On the first Thursday night in May, Bruin Wayne Cashman scored twice as Boston outshot the Blues 46-21, and outscored them 4-1. Now the Bruins were within one of winning the coveted Cup.

It had been a long season. It was Sunday afternoon, Mother's Day. The sun in Boston was hot and bright as the winter warriors met for the fourth game of the playoff finals. The match was nationally televised and St. Louis roused themselves for one last stand.

Jacques Plante had been driven from the nets early in the first game by a shot from Fred Stanfield's stick. Although the puck struck Plante on the mask, it still knocked him unconscious. Now, the acrobatic Glenn Hall, a man so nervous he frequently was sick before games, was playing goal for St. Louis. In the sixth minute of the first period Bruin defenseman Rick Smith ripped a 45-foot shot that somehow escaped Hall and the Bruins led 1-0. The crowd of 14,835 fans began to celebrate. But Red Berenson, the St. Louis ace, batted a rebound past Gerry Cheevers in the last minute of the period to even the score.

Early in the second period, Gary Sabourin of St. Louis shot from 35 feet and it got through Cheevers to put the Blues ahead. Esposito then took a face-off from Andre Boudrias and swiftly snapped a high shot over Hall's shoulder to tie the score 2-2 late in the period.

The teams went to their dressing rooms weary. This game was a struggle. The Blues seemed to get tougher as the series wore on. Seconds after the third period opened, the Blues' Larry Keenan took a pass from Phil Goyette and ripped it past Cheevers to put St. Louis back in front. The Bruin fans and players seemed stunned.

St. Louis went into a conservative defensive game, a style they played very well. They checked closely and carefully, taking few chances. Again and again the Bruins bore in on the goal, but again and again Glenn Hall turned them back. He made a series of spectacular saves, leaping and diving in front of his net and always deflecting the puck.

The crowd noise grew and grew. With less than seven minutes to play, the tireless, hustling McKenzie got his stick on the puck to the side of the goal and shot it across the goal-mouth as captain Johnny Bucyk moved in front. Bucyk shoved his stick at the puck and it shot past Hall and into the twine, bringing the red light on. The score was tied 3-3 and the crowd was on its feet screaming.

Despite desperate final bids by both teams, the score remained tied through the end of regulation time. During the regular season, it would have ended this way, in a tie. In the playoffs, however, games continue in sudden-death overtime—the first team to score wins. After a short intermission the two sides wearily resumed their warfare.

Sanderson won the mid-ice face-off for Boston and shot the puck into the Blues' end. Orr daringly rushed after it. The Blues tried to clear the puck to their offensive zone but Orr stole it off the stick of

Keenan and backhanded it along the backboards to
Sanderson, who was behind the Blues' net. Orr then
broke for the net. Sanderson flipped the puck over a
defender's stick and right back to Bobby, who was
skating past the goal from right to left. Orr wristed
the puck at the goal, just as defenseman Noel Picard
jammed his stick between Bobby's legs. As the puck
shot by goalie Hall, Orr went flying through the air,
his stick held high in his right hand. As the red light
flashed on, he crashed to the ice. His ecstatic teammates swarmed around him and the crowd stood
roaring in celebration. Paper streamers poured from
the rafters. The Bruins had won and the Stanley
Cup was theirs.

Bobby Orr is about to hit the ice as he is tripped after scoring the winning goal (left). Above, his jubilant teammates mob him.

The Bruins skated around the ice, sticks raised in triumph, receiving the tribute of the crowd. The disappointed Blues watched dejectedly, but tradition required that they remain, form a single line and exchange handshakes with their conquerors.

A golden carpet was rolled onto the ice and NHL president Clarence Campbell presented the Stanley Cup to Bruin captain Johnny Bucyk. The injured defenseman, Ted Green, who had been unable to play all season, touched the Cup and began to cry.

Bucyk raised the Cup high and skated around the rink with it as the cheers and applause continued.

Esposito had scored a record 13 goals and assisted on 14 others in the 14 games to top all scorers with 27 points. Orr had nine goals and 11 assists, Bucyk 11 goals and eight assists. The Bruins had won the last ten games in a row, sweeping series from both Chicago and St. Louis. The triumph was worth $7,500 per player to the Bruins. But statistics and money seemed unimportant at that moment.

These Bruins had won the Cup and Boston's first National Hockey League championship in 29 years —that was what mattered. Into the dressing room Orr sipped champagne from the Cup. Then it was passed to Esposito and the others. As these bone-tired, sweat-stained professionals laughed and yelled and hugged one another and wept unashamedly, the Cup, the symbol of their victory, was passed from hand to hand.

A dynasty appeared to be dawning. But in 1971, after Phil Esposito and Orr led Boston to their first regular-season title in 30 years, the Bruins were upset by Montreal in the Cup semifinals.

But the Bruins fought back, winning another divisional title in 1972. After trouncing Toronto and St. Louis in the early rounds of the playoffs, they faced a strong New York team in the finals.

Again, Bobby Orr made the big difference. Although he played with a serious knee injury, he set a new playoff record by making 19 assists. The Rangers, also plagued with injuries, fought gamely, but the Bruins were too strong, winning the intense, fight-filled series in six games. Boston had proved that it was still the team to beat for the coveted Cup in the 1970s.

2. Turnaround by Toronto

In the 1942 Stanley Cup playoffs, a team did something that no other team has ever done in one of the most dramatic playoff series in history.

In the middle of the 1941–42 season Pearl Harbor was bombed and the United States entered World War II. Canada had already been at war for two years. By the end of the season many of the NHL's finest players were serving in the armed forces. But hockey continued in the NHL although many of the players were aging veterans or untried rookies.

There were then seven teams in the NHL and the top six made the playoffs. The top two met in the opening round. The New York Rangers had captured the 1942 pennant by only three points in a close race with Toronto. But the Maple Leafs upset the Rangers in six games in the opening playoff round. Meanwhile, third-place Boston eliminated fourth-place Chicago and fifth-place Detroit eliminated sixth-place Montreal. Then Detroit upset Boston to gain the finals against Toronto.

So the finals featured second-place Toronto against fifth-place Detroit. The Red Wings had lost more games than they won during the regular season, but the team had some good players. Their leading scorer over the 48-game regular season had been Don Grosso with 23 goals. Sid Abel had scored 18. Black Jack Stewart was the backbone of a tough defense in front of goalie Johnny Mowers.

The Leafs had a star-studded team. They had a swift wing, Gordie Drillon, who had drilled 23 goals. And their captain was the league's all-star center, Syl Apps, who had scored 18. Sweeney Schriner had tallied 20. Drillon and Bucko McDonald on defense and Turk Broda in goal were second-team all-stars. Broda was at his best when it counted the most.

Detroit's Red Wings were underdogs to the mighty Maple Leafs, but they weren't intimidated. Their manager and coach, Jack Adams, said, "We

Young Turk Broda lets the puck get by him and into the goal.

may not have the greatest hockey club in the world, but we're loaded with fighting heart, and if there's anything that wins championships it's just that."

Adams and his opposing coach, Hap Day, were to go down in hockey history among the game's greatest leaders. Day was in his rookie season as a coach and he had reminded his players all year that Toronto had not won the Cup in ten years.

Toronto had the first two games at home, at Maple Leaf Gardens, and the Leafs figured as strong favorites. "We're not short of heart, ourselves," growled Day when he heard Adams' comment.

In the first game Detroit's Grosso, called "The Count," counted two goals and Sid Abel scored once as the Wings surprised the Leafs 3-2. In the second game Grosso scored twice more and Mud Bruneteau and Jim Brown each had one as the Wings shocked the Leafs with a second win, 4-3. Toronto's Apps and Drillon had been blanked in both games. The Leafs had been checked heavily by the tough Red Wings. When the Leafs left the ice, some of their fans booed them. And the next day they read criticisms of the team by Toronto sportswriters, who were deeply disappointed that their heroes were losing to a bunch of fifth-placers.

The teams moved to Detroit for the third game. Toronto tried to retaliate for what it considered rough tactics by Detroit in the first two games. Maple Leaf Turk Broda slashed Eddie Wares with his stick as the Wing skated across the goaltender's crease, putting the forward out of action. Then Detroit's Sid Abel was benched with an injury. Even with the rough play by Toronto referee Norman

Lampert gave six penalties to Detroit and only two to Toronto in both the first and third periods. But the Wings overcame injuries and penalties as defenseman Eddie Bush scored one goal and assisted on four others. In the first period Lorne Carr scored twice in 30 seconds for Toronto while the Wings were shorthanded. But the Leafs did not score again and lost 5-2.

Angered by the officials' calls, Detroit's Adams vowed to sweep his rivals with a fourth straight victory. Hap Day was desperate. He announced that he was benching two of his stars, Drillon and McDonald, and moving the Metz brothers, Don and Nick, into regular roles. He received a simple but touching letter from a 14-year-old girl fan from Toronto and used it to encourage his dispirited team. The girl wrote that she remained confident they would win and would pray for them. Day read the letter to his team before the game and it seemed to move them. Veteran Schriner announced, "Don't worry about this one, coach. We'll win it for the little girl."

However, Detroit drove to a quick 2-0 lead as Bruneteau scored in the second minute and Abel in the tenth minute. The Leafs seemed doomed. Here, however, their courage came through. Rugged Bob Davidson broke through to score for Toronto to cut the deficit to one goal. Then Carr scored one to tie the contest. Early in the third period Detroit's Carl Lipscombe unloaded a 35-foot blazer that fooled Broda and put the Wings on top once more, 3-2.

Now, with 13,694 fans cheering for the home team, with less than 15 minutes to play, behind by a goal in the game and by three games in the series, the Leafs' cause truly seemed hopeless. Still, they took the fight to the Wings, skating furiously, fighting desperately for the puck. Suddenly the Leafs' splendid Syl Apps cut gracefully in front of the net and with his wrists snapped the hard rubber disc past the goaltender to even the struggle with his first score of the series.

Toronto's players took heart. Detroit's players seemed to sag. Back came Apps, with slick moves on skates and cleverness with his stick. He slipped the puck to Don Metz, who passed it on to brother Nick, who knifed it through a narrow opening to beat the Wings' goalie. The Leafs led 4-3 and pranced on the ice in joy. Less than eight minutes were left.

Detroit bore in on Broda repeatedly in a determined effort to even the game. But referee Mel Harwood called four penalties on Grosso, Wares and other key Wings in the final minutes to finish off their hopes.

As the final siren sounded, the Leafs were yet alive and the Wings had been denied the clincher. Grosso and Wares, frustrated and angry, skated over to block referee Harwood's exit from the ice. Red Wing coach Jack Adams jumped off the bench and slipped and slid across the ice to join Grosso and Wares and a group of Detroit fans who were gathering around the referee.

Grosso and Wares were protesting the official's calls bitterly. But when Adams arrived he began to throw punches at Harwood. Some of the fans joined in. There nearly was a riot before attendants and police separated the participants and restored order.

Police had to provide escorts for referee Harwood and the president of the National Hockey League, Frank Calder, so they could leave the stadium safely.

From his hotel room that night, President Calder fined Grosso and Wares and suspended Adams, forbidding him to coach Detroit in the remaining games. A defenseman, Ebbie Goodfellow, had to assume the coaching chores of the Wings as the two teams returned to Toronto.

The Leafs had snatched a victory from the jaws of defeat. The Stanley Cup remained within their reach, although hardly at their fingertips. They were still down three games to one. In the fifth game, back on home ice, the newly formed line of Apps and the Metz brothers scored six goals and the Leafs destroyed disorganized Detroit 9-3. For Maple Leaf fans, the revenge was sweet.

The sixth game was played back in Detroit. If only they could pull themselves together, the Wings still had a big advantage. This time the hero was Turk Broda, the Leafs' amazing goalie. He was a high-living, fun-loving fellow who could be undependable in ordinary games, but was at his very best under pressure. Hockey enthusiasts say that if one game were played to decide the greatest hockey players, Turk Broda would be the toughest goalie.

Neither team scored in the first period, but Don Metz broke the scoreless tie with a goal in the second period to put Toronto ahead 1-0. Bob Goldham and Billy Taylor added goals in the last period to wrap up a 3-0 Toronto triumph. Broda had shut out the Red Wings and the series was even.

Broda slides out and kicks the puck away.

Toronto was the scene of the seventh and final game. Everything depended on one contest now. Detroit was due to win after losing three in a row, but Toronto had the advantage of playing on home ice.

The city of Toronto was gripped by the game. The townspeople could talk of little else. There were almost as many radio reports on this game as there were on the war. On that Saturday night in mid-April excited ticket-holders streamed into Maple Leaf Gardens and packed the place to the rafters. There were 16,218 persons there, a record hockey crowd for Canada at that time, and they roared

Rookie Pete Langelle raises his stick after scoring the winning goal for the Maple Leafs.

from the moment the puck was first dropped on the white ice. The players were battling for the puck, the game, the series and the Stanley Cup.

The two teams dueled defensively on even terms through an exciting but scoreless first period. In the

second period Detroit's Syd Howe shocked the home
crowd by skating and stickhandling a swift path
through the Leafs to score the first goal of the game,
putting Detroit on top 1-0.

The Wings protected their narrow margin with

passion, but the Leafs were a comeback team. They put on the pressure through the first part of a furious third period, and after seven minutes, Sweeney Schriner shot past Mowers to tie the game. The Toronto fans were on their feet cheering.

The goal and the tumult seemed to stun Detroit. The blue-jerseyed Leafs swarmed all over them in the last period, until Pete Langelle, a 24-year-old Maple Leaf playing his first full major league season, drove in and whipped the winning goal home.

Shortly thereafter, Schriner, a 30-year-old veteran, slammed his second goal of the game past Mowers to make the score 3-1. Big Broda was as impassable as a boulder for the rest of the game and at the final siren Toronto had a 3-1 victory. They had won the Cup in four straight games after losing the first three.

Three years later, in 1945, Toronto and Detroit met again in the Stanley Cup final. This time their roles were reversed. Turk Broda was in the armed forces, but Toronto's rookie goaltender, Frank McCool, a nervous, scholarly youngster, shut out Detroit in the first three games, 1-0, 2-0 and 1-0, a shutout record in final playoffs. Then in a wild fourth game Detroit avoided disgrace, winning 5-3.

Inspired, Harry Lumley, Detroit's fine young netminder, turned around and blanked Toronto twice in a row for 2-0 and 1-0 Detroit victories. Suddenly Detroit was on the verge of duplicating Toronto's comeback of 1942.

But in the Sunday night final in Detroit, after the two teams had battled to a 1-1 tie late in the game, Toronto's Babe Pratt blasted the puck past Lumley

Another great Toronto goalie, Frank McCool, guards the nets.

from his defense position to win the game 2-1. The Maple Leafs had barely missed losing the Cup to the Red Wings after winning the first three games of the series.

But these two comebacks—Toronto's in 1942 and Detroit's in 1945—were the most heroic in the history of Stanley Cup finals play. As both teams had learned, when the Cup is at stake, the series is not over until the final siren has ended the final game.

3. Saga of the Silver Fox

Many families have been important to the history of hockey. But none has contributed as much over so long a period as the Patricks. Already in 1911, the Patrick brothers, Lester and Frank, were completing their careers as players and becoming hockey businessmen. They built the first artificial ice plants in Canada for the Vancouver and Victoria teams of the Pacific Coast League, which they helped to start. The Vancouver arena was the largest in hockey at the time, seating 10,000.

Over the years, Frank Patrick introduced the use of numbers on players' jerseys, developed the system of post-season playoffs which still is followed in hockey, and devised 22 hockey rules that are still in effect in the NHL. He was a manager with the Boston Bruins and became an official of the National Hockey League in the 1930s.

Lester became the manager and coach of the New York Rangers in 1926. Many old-time hockey fans believe he was the greatest coach of all time.

Lester Patrick had two sons. Lynn was an outstanding forward with the Rangers for ten seasons and

Lester Patrick in 1940.

Muzz was a defenseman with the Rangers for five seasons. Both Lynn and Muzz later managed and coached the Rangers. Lynn later managed the Boston Bruins, then became general manager and coach of the St. Louis Blues. Muzz became an official with Madison Square Garden in New York, the home of the Rangers.

Of all the Patricks, Lester was perhaps the most remarkable. He was tall and gaunt, a tough player and an inspirational and imaginative leader. Shortly after the New York Rangers were organized, he was hired to manage and coach the club. New York already had a hockey team—the Americans. But during Patrick's years, the Rangers became the more popular team. The Americans went out of business in 1942.

In their very first season, 1926-27, Patrick's Rangers captured the pennant in the American Division of the NHL. The league then had 10 teams in two divisions—American and Canadian. But the Rangers were eliminated by Boston in the first round of the Stanley Cup playoffs. In their second season they finished second to Boston, but the playoffs were a different story.

The Rangers had a classic club which included some of the outstanding stars in the history of the sport—Bill and Bun Cook, Frank Boucher, Ching Johnson, Murray Murdoch, Taffy Abel and a strong, splendid goaltender, Lorne Chabot.

The Rangers squeezed past Pittsburgh's Yellow Jackets in the opening round of the playoffs, then upset Boston's Bruins in the semi-finals. The Montreal Maroons, a second team in Montreal at the time, had knocked off the Canadiens and Ottawa in the Canadian division, so the Rangers and the Maroons met in the finals.

The Rangers were forced to play all the games away from home, at the Forum in Montreal, the home of the Maroons, because a circus was appearing in Madison Square Garden in New York. Thus the odds were against the Rangers. The Maroons had a good team, including Nels Stewart, one of the great players of all time, Hooley Smith, Babe Siebert and a superb goalie, Clint Benedict.

In the opener of the best-three-of-five finals, Benedict blanked the Rangers and the Maroons triumphed 2-0. In the second game, both goalies were shutting out their foes in the second period. Then Nels Stewart sliced through the Ranger defense and wristed a hard, rising shot right at Chabot. The puck struck him with terrible force close to his left eye, felling him. In those days no goalie in professional hockey wore a mask and injuries were common. Chabot lay on the ice, unconscious and bleeding. He was rushed to Royal Victoria Hospital, where it was found he had a severe concussion and would be sidelined for the series.

In these days, teams carried only one goaltender. Usually, there was someone else in the arena—a trainer, a retired player or a young prospect—who was available to go into the nets if the goalie was injured. But the opposing team had to give its approval. If approval was not granted, another player on the team's roster had to fill in.

Since only one goalie was ready to play, the two teams retired to the dressing room while someone else got ready for the Rangers. Coach Patrick had two goaltenders in the stands available for relief duty—Alex Connell, the netminder for the Ottawa team in the NHL, and Hughie McCormick, the netminder for London, Ontario, in the Canadian Pro League. Patrick sent word to Maroons manager

Eddie Gerard that he wished to use Connell.

Six years earlier, Patrick had done a big favor for Eddie Gerard. Patrick's Vancouver team was playing the Toronto St. Pats for the Stanley Cup. Vancouver won two of the first three games because the Toronto defense had suffered a series of crippling injuries.

The St. Pats' manager, Charlie Querrie, approached Patrick for permission to use Eddie Gerard, who played for an Ontario team which had finished its season. Patrick graciously gave his permission. Gerard seemed to make the difference. The St. Pats won the next two games and took the Stanley Cup. Gerard had so much fun in his unexpected chance to help win a Cup that he refused any salary. He accepted only a diamond stickpin as a souvenir of the occasion.

Now this same Gerard was managing the Maroons and he had to give Patrick permission to use a reserve goalie. Patrick might have expected him to repay the earlier favor. But Gerard was a tough man. He saw that he had the Rangers in trouble and he didn't intend to do them any favors. He sent back a note: "Hell no, you can't use Connell."

Patrick sent back a note asking to use McCormick. And Gerard returned this message: "Forget it. Play goal yourself."

Now Patrick was in a rage. He told the team his problem and asked for volunteers. No one volunteered. Instead, Frank Boucher said jokingly, "Why *don't* you play goal?"

And Patrick snapped, "All right, I'll do it!" The team had been allowed only ten minutes to make the change and the time was almost gone. He hurriedly began to strap on the bulky goalkeeper's pads. Some of his players tried to talk him out of it, but Patrick's mind was made up. Chabot's pads and skates were too big for him. He looked ridiculous when he was dressed, but he was ready.

Patrick was 45 years old and had not played a minute of hockey for seven years. In all his professional career he had only played goal for a few minutes. His hair was gray and he was out of shape. He was tough and courageous, but he admitted later that he was scared and nervous. This was the Stanley Cup finals. He would be facing some of the sport's fiercest shooters in front of a huge crowd of enemy fans.

"I'll do the best I can," he said. "You guys just check. Don't let them get off many shots. If I make a save, get back and clear the puck for me. Play hard and maybe we'll surprise them."

The Montreal fans were surprised when Patrick skated out awkwardly and took his place in the Ranger net. The Rangers hit a few practice shots at him, but they were afraid to shoot very hard. Then referee Mike Rodden said, "Let's go," and the game resumed.

The Rangers played like madmen. They pursued the puck with passion. They tried to break up every Montreal offensive play before it began. And for a while they succeeded. But the Maroons figured they had an old man at their mercy and they fought with determination of their own.

Russ Oatman ripped a shot for the Maroons. Patrick ducked and it sailed past his ear and over the net. Bill Phillips punched a shot right at Patrick and the old man caught it. Oatman drove another at Patrick, but it bounced off his pads. Jimmy Ward shot, but Lester stopped it. Babe Siebert shot, but Lester stopped it.

The siren sounded. Somehow Patrick had shut out the Maroons through the remaining part of the second period and the game remained scoreless. In their dressing room at intermission, the Rangers seemed to take heart. Perhaps this daring gamble would work after all. At least they would go down fighting.

The Rangers roared out and in the first minute of the third period Cook lashed a long shot that got by the Maroon goalie and the Rangers took a 1-0 lead. But the Rangers were still not out of danger. The spectacular Stewart pounded at Patrick. "Ol' Poison," as he was called, drove the puck off Patrick's pads, then sizzled one off his stick. Finally, with less than six minutes left, he faked a shot and Patrick went down to block it. Then Stewart lifted the puck into the net to tie the game.

Surely, Patrick would crack. Since he was out of shape, every minute made it more likely. But he did not. The Maroons continued to fire away and somehow he stopped them through the remainder of regulation time. But the Rangers had not scored either.

Now the teams went into overtime. Patrick— nicknamed "The Silver Fox"—was exhausted. It seemed only a matter of time before he had to be beat. The Rangers were playing defensively to protect him, and the Maroons were applying most of the pressure. Stewart shot one, two, three, four times

The great Nels Stewart, who nearly defeated old goalie Lester Patrick and later starred for the Boston Bruins.

and failed. Dunc Munro unleashed a long shot that Lester managed to smother.

Suddenly, the Rangers' Ching Johnson got his stick on the puck and broke up ice along with Frank Boucher. Maroon goalie Benedict came out to defend against Johnson, but Johnson passed to Boucher, and Boucher banged the puck into the nets. At 7:05 of the first overtime, the Rangers had won 2-1.

The Rangers rushed to Patrick. He began to cry as they carried him from the ice. The Montreal fans were shocked by the surprising ending, but they stood and cheered Patrick as he was carried off.

He insisted later, "I stopped maybe six hard shots altogether. The boys backchecked terrifically to save the old man." But he had handled 18 shots, some 15 of which were considered dangerous, and had stopped his foes three different times when the Rangers were shorthanded because of a penalty. Stewart later said, "The old white-haired son of a gun was terrific."

In the rest of the series the Rangers seemed inspired by Patrick's performance. Joe Miller was brought in to man the nets (Gerard gave permission this time). He was beaten 2-0 when the series resumed three nights later. But he came back to win 1-0, tying the series at two victories each. The winner of the fifth game would take home the Stanley Cup.

Early in the final game, Miller fell on an outstretched stick and was hurt. For a few minutes it seemed Patrick or someone else might have to go into the nets in another emergency. But Miller received first aid and carried on gallantly.

The brilliant Frank Boucher blasted in a goal to give the Rangers the lead, 1-0. A tying goal by Montreal was disallowed by referee Rodden, who ruled the Maroons had been offside on the play. The Maroons disagreed. Their fans threw trash onto the ice and booed the official.

The Maroons finally scored, but Boucher banged in another goal for the Rangers. They protected their 2-1 lead to the last siren. Patrick led New York onto the ice to take possession of the Stanley Cup. The disappointed Montreal fans were no longer cheering Patrick—they were ready to attack referee Rodden and league president Calder because of the call on the disputed "offside" goal. The referee escaped out a side door, while the president locked himself in an office and waited until tempers calmed.

Meanwhile, all was celebration in the Ranger dressing room. If ever a team and a coach deserved a trophy, the Rangers and valiant Lester Patrick deserved the Stanley Cup that year.

4. Sudden-Death

In the late 1930s and early 1940s, the teams to reckon with in the NHL were the Boston Bruins and the New York Rangers. The two teams were involved in some of the greatest Stanley Cup playoffs in memory—and the one thing these playoffs had in common was the element of the sudden-death overtime.

The Bruins had won their last Stanley Cup in 1929. Then in 1938, nine years later, they finished first in their division in the regular season. Suddenly Boston fans were hopeful that the Bruins would win the cup again. Then disaster struck. Boston was eliminated in the first round of the playoffs in three straight games.

Manager and coach Art Ross had assembled an awesome array of players headed up by Bill Cowley and "The Kraut Line"—Milt Schmidt, Woody Dumart and Bobby Bauer. Others who shone on offense were Roy Conacher and Art Jackson. Eddie Shore and Dit Clapper anchored the defense.

Shore was 36 years old and in his 13th season in the NHL. Small, but tough, he had brawled his way

47

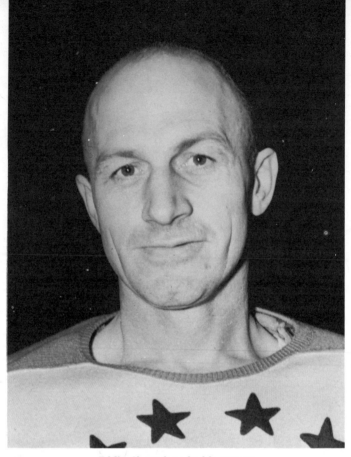

Eddie Shore late in his career.

to the all-star team seven times and to the Most Valuable Player award four times. He had survived 900 stitches in his face, head and body and fractures of his back, hip and collarbone. His jaw had been broken five times, his nose 14 times, and every tooth had been knocked from his mouth.

Going into the 1938–39 season, Shore was fading, but he was still considered "the Babe Ruth of Hockey," the man who had drawn thousands of fans to this swift and fierce game. With him on Boston's back line was stylish Dit Clapper, who at 32 was in his 12th NHL campaign. Behind them at goal was 10-year veteran Tiny Thompson, a four-time winner of the Vezina Trophy as best goalie in the league.

Early in the 1938–39 season, manager Art Ross made a bold move, selling Thompson to Detroit and bringing up a 23-year-old American-born rookie, Frank Brimsek, to tend the nets. Players, press and fans were startled and outraged. Thompson's roommate, Dit Clapper, threatened to retire. But in his first three weeks, the brilliant Brimsek scored six shutouts in a stretch of seven games. Critics of Ross were convinced and Brimsek became known as "Mr. Zero." By season's end, he had won the Calder Trophy as rookie of the year and the Vezina Trophy as most effective goaltender.

By the end of the 1938–39 regular season, the Bruins had lost only 10 of 48 games and won the pennant from the Rangers by 16 points. Cowley had won the scoring championship and Most Valuable Player award. Cowley and Clapper were on the first all-star team, while Brimsek, Bauer and Dumart had made the second. The Bruins were burning to capture the Cup. Ross growled, "We won't be denied this time."

They opened the playoffs with a best-four-of-seven series against the Rangers. The Rangers had fallen on hard times after their Stanley Cup victory in 1928. But now they were back. Lester Patrick was still general manager and former star Frank Boucher was coach. The team included Patrick's two sons, Lynn and Muzz, Neil and Mac Colville, Clint Smith, Phil Watson, and goalies Davey Kerr and Bert Gardiner.

The opener was played in the old Madison Square Garden in New York. The two teams were tied 1-1 at the end of regulation time. They struggled scoreless through the first overtime and the second.

In the last minute of the third overtime, Bruin star Bill Cowley eluded Muzz Patrick, cut into a corner and sent a perfect pass to Mel Hill, who was camped in front of Ranger goalie Davey Kerr. Hill knocked the puck past Kerr for the 2-1 victory at 19:25 of the period and 119:25 of the game. It was 1:10 a.m. when the Bruins skated off in triumph.

The teams moved to Boston's Garden for the second and third games. The second game was 2-2 at the end of regulation play. Near the midway mark of the first overtime, Cowley led Hill with a pass and Mel stroked it past Gardiner, who had taken over the New York net, for a 3-2 win. Hill had two straight sudden-death goals. Boston fans went wild.

Who was this Hill? Ironically, he had tried out for the Rangers before the 1937–38 season. They thought he was "too small" and turned him away. He had caught on with the Bruins, but during 1938–39 had tallied only ten goals.

In the third game, the discouraged Rangers were a soft touch, losing again to the Bruins 4-1. They returned to New York one loss away from elimination. But Patrick and coach Boucher fired them up. In front of a wild-eyed Ranger crowd of 15,692, the Rangers carried the battle to the Bruins in a savage struggle.

The game didn't begin hopefully. After 49 seconds of play Bruin Milt Schmidt batted the puck out of a

Ranger goalie Davey Kerr and Lynn Patrick defend the goal against the Bruins' Bobby Bauer during the 1939 playoffs.

scramble at the goal-mouth and into the goal. Then eight minutes later Ranger Mac Colville beat Brimsek to even the struggle at 1-1.

In the second period the Rangers struck suddenly and surprisingly when they were shorthanded because of a penalty. Lynn Patrick banked the puck into the nets off a Bruin skate at 10:02 to put New York ahead 2-1.

Shore, playing with a broken nose suffered in a fight during the first period, spearheaded repeated Bruin attacks from then to the finish, but goaltender Gardiner repelled every shot and the Rangers had the victory.

Back in Boston for the fifth game, the bitter rivals battled in a 1-1 tie in regulation time. This time a Ranger was the hero. Clint "Snuffy" Smith beat Bruin goalie Brimsek at 17:19 to decide the game in

New York's favor. Then in New York, the Rangers prevailed 3-1 for their third straight victory. The series was squared at three triumphs apiece. The teams returned to Boston for the deciding contest.

The old arena was filled to the rafters with Bruin fans. The two teams fought once again to a 1-1 tie in regulation time. The first overtime period was scoreless. So was the second. The tension grew as the skaters struggled into the third extra session. Each shot brought the crowd to its feet. Each save brought a roar or a groan from the fans.

Late in the period Eddie Shore took the puck and passed it to Conacher on the fly. Conacher let fly a shot at Ranger goalie Bert Gardiner, who grabbed the puck and tossed it into a corner. The Bruins' Cowley beat the Rangers to it and flipped it in front of the New York net.

There stood Mel Hill.

He slapped the rubber disc past the startled Ranger goalie and into the nets. After 108 minutes of hockey the Bruin fans had their victory. They cheered themselves hoarse as the players crowded around Mel Hill. Forever after, he was known as Mel "Sudden Death" Hill. He even signed autographs that way.

Boston went into the finals against Toronto and won four out of five, finally capturing the Cup once again. Ironically, their one loss was the only overtime game of the finals.

This brilliant Boston team suffered a setback during the following season. Eddie Shore was traded to the New York Americans. Although Schmidt, Bauer, Dumart and Cowley finished as the first four scorers in the circuit, and the Bruins finished first, the Rangers gained revenge in the opening round of the playoffs. Goalie Davey Kerr blanked the Bruins three times and the Rangers won the series in six games. The Rangers went into the best-of-seven finals against Toronto. They won the first game, 2-1, at 15:30 of the first overtime. Alf Pike scored to win. Then they routed Toronto 6-2 in the second game. All the rest of the games would be played in Toronto.

But in Maple Leaf Gardens Toronto squared the series with 2-1 and 3-0 triumphs. In the fifth game

"Sudden Death" Hill (left) smiles after playoff victory.

Bryan Hextall (far left) raises his stick in triumph after scoring the overtime goal that won the Cup for New York in 1940.

the Rangers found themselves back in overtime, tied 1-1. Muzz Patrick was the new hero—he slammed in the decider after 11:43 of the first extra session for the Rangers' second overtime victory of the series. The Rangers led three games to two.

In the sixth game, shaking off the taunts of enemy fans, the Rangers fought to a 2-2 tie at the end of regulation time. Incredibly, they faced yet another overtime. This one didn't last long. At 2:07 of the overtime Bryan Hextall snapped the disc past the Maple Leafs' great goalie, Turk Broda, for the 3-2 triumph. The Rangers claimed the Cup and held their celebration in an arena of departing, disappointed fans. This was the Rangers' third overtime

triumph of the finals, reversing their disappointing series of the season before.

The Bruins were far from through. The following season, 1940–41, they set records which still endure. They went 23 consecutive games without a defeat, and lost only eight games all season, winning their fourth straight pennant by five points from Toronto. They entered the 1941 playoffs poised to prove they were the real champions.

Toronto was a formidable foe in the first round. The teams traded games until they had two apiece. Then in Boston, the Leafs' Pete Langelle tallied at 17:31 of overtime to give the Leafs a 2-1 triumph and a three-to-two lead in games. Boston had its back to the wall, one game from elimination. But the Bruins got back, winning the sixth game 2-1.

And so the teams met in Boston for the seventh and deciding game. The teams tied the score at 1-1. And who settled it? Mel Hill, who was little more than a sub by then. This time Hill didn't need sudden death. He poked the puck past Broda in regulation time for the 2-1 triumph.

Hill, one of the more unlikely heroes in hockey history, had convinced Bostonians that the Bruins were a team of destiny. In the finals, they swept the Detroit Red Wings in four straight games to take the Stanley Cup for the second time in three years.

What Boston hockey fans could not foresee was that their era was over. The Bruins did not win the Cup again for nearly thirty years. For the hapless Rangers the wait would be longer still.

5. The Rocket Blasts Off

Montreal was playing Toronto in the second game of the first round in the 1944 Stanley Cup playoffs. The Canadiens had lost the first game but one man was determined that they would not lose another. Dark eyes blazing, black hair flying, his muscular body throwing defenders off as they sought to contain him, Maurice "Rocket" Richard blasted Toronto off the ice.

In the second minute of the second period, Montreal defenseman Mike McMahon led Richard with a pass and the Rocket roared in from the right wing firing the puck past Paul Bibeault into the Toronto net. Fifteen seconds later his wingmates, Elmer Lach and Toe Blake, set Richard up again and he ripped the puck past the goalie again. Before the period was over, he drove through defenders and drove the disc into the nets a third time to complete the hat trick— three goals in one game.

But he was not finished. One minute into the third period, the Rocket sizzled a slapshot from outside which slammed past the Leaf goalie and into the net with frightening force. Three minutes later,

Richard and Blake tore free on a breakaway. Richard took a pass from Blake and arched the puck perfectly into a narrow opening left unguarded by the frustrated goaltender.

Richard had scored five goals in just over twenty minutes of play in an unprecedented playoff performance. The Canadiens won 5-1. After the game, a voice on the public address system announced the three leading players of the game. Usually two men are chosen from the winning team and one from the losers. But that night the choices were "Richard . . . Richard . . . and Richard!"

Richard was not the first hockey superstar to shine for Montreal. In fact the Canadiens, the "home team" for French-Canadians, had a long tradition of spectacular hockey. Richard's thunder brought back the glories of an earlier era in Canadien history and recalled the exploits of Howie Morenz—whose greatest gift was the speed of lightning.

Morenz, short and slender, never weighed more than 165 pounds, but he could fly. It was said that when he was skating at full speed he made his rivals seem to be going backwards. And he could do magical things with the puck. He was like a great broken-

Rocket Richard drives in for a shot.

field runner in football. Possibly no player in hockey history ever carried the puck so spectacularly through the opposition to score with quick, hard, accurate shots. One season he scored 40 goals in a 44-game schedule.

Many regard him as the greatest player of all time. He was also a spectacular personality, who changed fancy suits two and three times a day, lived high and enjoyed life.

With the jaunty Auriel Joliat, Billy Boucher, and Georges Vezina in goal, Morenz sparked the red, blue and white Canadiens to their first Stanley Cup in 1924. The playoff series were short in those days and the Canadiens eliminated three foes in six games. Morenz scored seven goals.

Led by Morenz and Joliat, the Canadiens won regular-season championships in 1928, 1929, 1931 and 1932. But they frequently and frustratingly fell short in playoff pressure. They won the Stanley Cup only twice between 1928 and 1932.

In 1929 Montreal was swept out of the playoffs in three straight games in the first round. Then in 1929–30 they slipped to second place in the league standings. As they entered the 1930 playoffs their fans and critics were pessimistic.

In the first round they faced the Chicago Black Hawks in a two-game series that would be decided by who scored the most total goals. The Canadiens won the opener 1-0, but the Black Hawks "won" the second game, 2-1. Since each team had scored two goals in the series, the contest went into overtime. The first two overtime periods were scoreless. In the third extra session at 11:43, Morenz sped into the

Chicago zone and unleashed a bullet past goalie Charlie Gardiner. The Canadiens had won the series with three total goals to the Black Hawks' two.

In the best-of-three semi-finals against the Rangers, the Canadiens won the opener in the fourth overtime when Gus Rivers gunned in the winning goal for a 2-1 triumph. The Canadiens then finished off the series in the next game with a 2-0 victory. In the best-of-three finals, the Canadiens swept Boston's Bruins two straight, 3-0 and 4-3. Montreal had its second Stanley Cup.

The following season, 1930-31, the Canadiens won their third pennant in four years. In the first round of the playoffs they met Boston in a bitter battle. Boston won the opener 5-4 in overtime, and Montreal captured the second contest 1-0. Georges Mantha won the third game for Montreal 4-3 with a goal in the sixth minute of overtime. The Bruins bounced back to square the series at two victories each with a 3-1 triumph. The Canadiens qualified for the finals in the fifth game when Wildor Larochelle scored the winning goal after 19 minutes of overtime.

Montreal met Chicago in a best-of-five final series. The first two games would be played in Chicago and the rest in Montreal. The Canadiens captured the opener 2-1. But Morenz, Leduc and others were injured and Montreal was in trouble. Chicago won the second game 2-1 after 24:50 of overtime and the third game 3-2 after 53:50 of overtime to take the series lead.

Morenz and the others were pressed back into full service. The Canadiens squared the series with a 4-2

Canadien star Howie Morenz appears in a Black Hawk uniform late in his career.

victory in the fourth game. Then they won the series and the Stanley Cup with a 2-0 victory in the finale. Morenz scored the final goal and was escorted off the ice to the cheers of the crowd.

The Canadiens won another pennant in 1932, but failed in the playoffs. Morenz was gambling heavily and drinking. His legs started to give out and he was traded to Chicago in 1934. A year later Morenz moved on again, to the New York Americans. In 1936 he returned to Montreal, but the glory of his earlier years could not be recaptured.

Late in January 1937, in a game against Chicago, Morenz tripped over a stick and was checked into the boards, breaking his left leg in four places. Five weeks later, while recovering in a hospital, he collapsed and died of a brain hemorrhage. All Canada mourned his death. His body lay in state in the Montreal Forum. Thousands of fans passed his casket, many weeping.

Joseph Henri Maurice Richard came along five years later, gaining the attention of fans as only Morenz had done before. His only competition in the NHL came from Detroit's Gordie Howe. Howe was a great all-round player, and he was more durable than Richard. But the Rocket was more explosive and more colorful, one of the most exciting players in sports history.

In his last two seasons as an amateur, Richard had broken his ankle and his wrist. In his first season in the majors he broke his other ankle after only 16 games. Fearing he was injury-prone, the Canadiens actually offered to trade him to the Rangers but Ranger manager Lester Patrick turned down the deal.

Although many players were in the army during the mid-1940s, Richard's bad ankles kept him from army service. In his first full season he scored 32 goals and led the Canadiens to their first pennant in ten years.

Manager Tom Gorman had assembled an outstanding team for coach Dick Irvin. Richard joined Toe Blake and Elmer Lach in the famed "Punch Line." Kenny Reardon, Emile Bouchard, and Glen Harmon helped fill out the team.

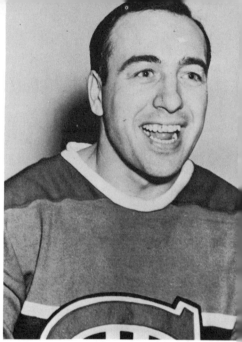

Elmer Lach and Toe Blake (top left and right) teamed with Rocket Richard to form the "Production Line." At right is ace goalie Bill Durnan.

The Montreal goaltender was Bill Durnan. He broke into the NHL as a 29-year-old rookie in 1943–44 and won the Vezina trophy. The 6-foot-2, 210-pounder used both hands equally well and soon awed the Canadiens' opponents.

Durnan was the base on which this mighty Montreal team of 1943–44 was built, but the Rocket was its spirit. Richard really was a left-hander, and coach Irvin observed that he had a brilliant backhand shot and was doubly difficult to defense going down the right side. Irvin converted the left-winger to right wing and the Canadiens were on their way. At the end of his first full season Richard played a classic Stanley Cup series.

The Canadiens had lost only 5 of their 50 games in the regular season, winning the pennant by a tremendous 25 points. They were heavily favored entering the playoffs. It was a shock when third-place Toronto upset them 3-1 in the first game of the first round. Then Richard shocked the Maple Leafs and the hockey world when he scored all five goals in Montreal's 5-1 victory. The Canadiens pressed their advantage, winning 2-1 and 4-1 in the next two games to take a commanding lead in the best-of-seven series.

Back in Montreal for the fifth game, the Rocket scored two goals, leading a goal-scoring spree that demolished the Leafs 11-0. The Canadiens scored five of the goals in only three minutes and 36 seconds. This spurt and their total of 11 goals both endure as modern playoff records. Montreal went on to the Cup finals against Chicago.

The series opened in Montreal where the Canadiens routed the Black Hawks 5-1. Then in Chicago, the Canadiens won 3-1 and 3-2. Richard got all three goals in the second game. Back in Montreal the Black Hawks battled back and led 4-1, but goals by the Rocket and Blake in the last five minutes sent the game into overtime. Toe Blake won the game at 9:12 of overtime. Montreal had swept the series.

Richard had scored a playoff record of 12 goals in the nine games. Sweat dripping from his tousled black hair, Richard drank champagne from the big bowl and said with a smile, "Thees ees sometheeng, no?"

More was to come. The following season Richard became the first player in the NHL ever to score 50 goals in a single season, setting this standard in just 50 games. The Canadiens lost only eight of the games and coasted to the pennant by 13 points. In the first round of the playoffs Richard scored six goals in the six games, but the Canadiens were upset by Toronto.

In 1946 Richard had his troubles, scoring only 27 goals. The Canadiens had their troubles, too, although they beat out Boston in a tight fight for the pennant. Then they exploded in the playoffs. In the first round they clobbered Chicago 6-2, 5-1, 8-2 and 7-2 in a fearful rout led once more by the Rocket.

The finals against the Bruins were much closer. The first two games were in Montreal. In the first, the score was tied 3-3 at 9:08 of overtime when Richard made a spectacular rink-long dash, faked the goalie out of position and scored on a sizzling shot. The second game also went into overtime and Montreal's Jimmy Peters scored the winning goal.

In Boston, the Bruins lost their third straight, 4-2. They came back, however, to win the fourth game in overtime. But back in Montreal for the fifth game the Canadiens won the Cup with a 6-3 romp led by

Maurice Rocket Richard was fierce in appearance and in behavior on the ice.

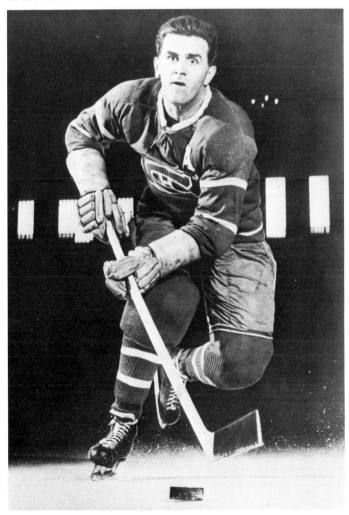

the Punch Line. Richard had scored seven goals in the playoffs and he kissed the Cup a second time.

The Canadiens captured their fourth straight pennant in 1947 as Richard scored 45 goals. In the first round of the playoffs they eliminated Boston in six vicious games, two of which went into overtime.

The finals against Toronto opened in Montreal. Durnan shut out the Leafs in the opener 6-0. The Leafs retaliated by riding Richard hard in the second game. In a collision with Gus Mortson, the Rocket tore ligaments in his knee, but continued to play. Later, in a rage, he began swinging at the Leafs with his stick and his fists, knocking down Vic Lynn and Bill Ezinicki. He was first given a major penalty, then thrown from the game. Toronto won 4-0. Later, he was fined and suspended for one game. He said, "I just lost my temper."

Possibly his temper lost the series for the Canadiens. In Toronto, the Leafs won 4-2 in the game that Richard missed and then won the next game 2-1 in overtime. The Canadiens came back to win the fifth game 3-1. But the Leafs won the sixth game and the Cup on a goal by Ted Kennedy. As the youthful Leafs celebrated, the aging Canadiens limped away. The old Canadiens were finished.

The Rocket and his Canadiens slipped from the spotlight for a while as Gordie Howe and the Red Wings rose to power. But the remarkable Richard would return from the shadows, surrounded by new stars, to write still another chapter in Stanley Cup history.

6. The Red Wings Fly High

It was March of 1950. Detroit and Toronto were playing a Stanley Cup semi-final series. The Red Wings' young Gordie Howe charged Toronto's Ted Kennedy to check him. But instead, he was struck by Kennedy's stick and as Kennedy sidestepped, he slammed headfirst into the sideboards. The crowd in Detroit's Olympia Stadium grew silent. Howe lay unconscious on the ice, a pool of blood spreading beneath his head.

He was carried off the ice on a stretcher and rushed to a hospital. He had a cut eyelid, a scratched eyeball, a broken nose, and a fractured cheekbone. Most important, he had suffered a fractured skull and possible brain damage. Yet as he was being wheeled into the operating room, he mumbled to manager Jack Adams, "I'm sorry I couldn't help you more tonight."

Howe underwent a 90-minute operation to relieve the pressure on his brain. For days he hovered between life and death. His mother was flown to Detroit to be by his bedside. Even if he lived, it seemed doubtful he ever would play again.

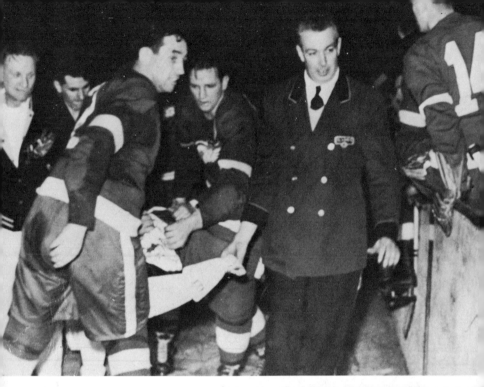

Gordie Howe is carried
off the ice after his in-
jury, above. At right, he
smiles from his hospital
bed a week later.

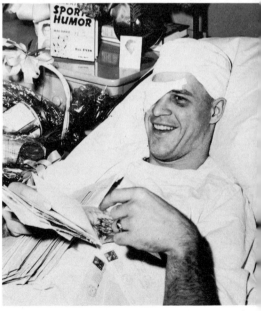

Amazingly, Gordie Howe recovered. Not only did he play again, he dominated his sport as no other athlete ever has dominated a game.

Most hockey experts consider Howe the best player of all time, if not the most exciting. He was 6-foot-2, and weighed 205 pounds. He came back from his almost fatal injury to play for 20 more years—an amazing record in itself. He was probably the strongest player ever to play the game and may have been the meanest, although off the ice he was gentlemanly, soft-spoken and friendly. On the ice, he used his stick like a weapon, threw off defenders, and punched so hard that even the roughest opponents seldom picked a fight more than once or twice.

Howe may also have been the smartest player and the smoothest player ever. He controlled the puck more often than anyone in memory. He was a great shooter—with both hands—but he was unselfish with the puck, becoming a great playmaker as well. Before he retired at the age of 43 after 25 years in the NHL, Howe held his sport's major records with 786 goals, 1,023 assists and 1,809 points in regular-season play. Including playoffs he had 853 goals, 1,114 assists and 1,967 points. He also was second to his old teammate Ted Lindsay in penalty minutes with 1,643 in regular-season play and 1,861 including playoffs. The mathematics of his history are marvelous, but the man behind them was even more remarkable.

He sat in the Detroit dressing room after a game one night near the end of his career. Perspiration streamed from his graying hair down his ruggedly handsome face. When he grinned, his front teeth were missing, long since knocked out in forgotten hockey battles.

He said, "I started out as a boy just wanting to play, and then I just wanted to be a pro. Then I just wanted to make the majors, and then I wanted more than anything to win a Stanley Cup. And now, here I am, all these years later, with all those records, and who'd have believed it? Twenty-five years behind me and now it's almost over, which is sad."

There was a cut on his cheek and another on his arm and a black and blue knot on his thigh. He still was strong, but he had aged past his prime. He remembered those good old days, though. He smiled and said, "I'll tell you, as much as my records mean to me, I'd give any of them up rather than give up one of those Stanley Cups we won. That was the big thing, winning the big mug. That's what counts— the team, and winning. And what I remember best are the nights we took the Cup."

Beginning even before Howe's injury, the Red Wings had assembled one of the two or three greatest teams in hockey history. Playing on Howe's line was "Terrible Ted" Lindsay, a smaller but equally fearless man. Playing at left wing, Lindsay scored 20 to 30 goals a season. In his 17 seasons he set the NHL record for penalty minutes with 1,808 in regular seasons and 2,002 including playoffs. Players do not win games for their teams sitting in the penalty box, but sometimes aggressiveness in hockey can be measured by penalty minutes. Lindsay and Howe put fear in foes.

Completing the famed "Production Line" was Sid Abel, the stylish center who later coached and managed the Red Wings. Abel's successor as the team's star center was Alex Delvecchio, a splendid performer who played for more than 20 years.

The key man on defense was almost as great a star as Howe—Leonard Patrick "Red" Kelly. Kelly was a swift and agile skater, a smart hockey player who rushed to 15 or more goals seven straight seasons and was six times an all-star. He ranks with Shore, Harvey and Orr among the best defensemen of all time. As mild-mannered as Howe and Lindsay were mean, Kelly four times won the Lady Byng Trophy for excellence and sportsmanlike conduct. He was so versatile that late in his 20-year career he converted to center and starred for Toronto.

At the beginning of the Red Wing reign, the goaltender was Harry Lumley and at the end it was Glenn Hall, who was just beginning a great career. But through most of Detroit's glory years the goalie was Terry Sawchuk, an intense, moody performer, who gave up an average of less than two goals a game five straight seasons. He lasted 21 seasons, playing 971 games in the nets and chalking up 102 shutouts, both records. He died tragically in 1970 after finishing that season in a New York Ranger uniform.

Jack Adams was the Red Wing manager who put this amazing team together and Tommy Ivan was the coach through its best years.

The Red Wing dynasty began by winning the regular-season title in 1949. The victory turned out to be the first of seven in a row, one of the most amazing strings in hockey. The string ended in 1955, but Detroit came back to win it in 1957. Twice in this stretch the Red Wings won 44 games, then the most wins ever in a 70-game schedule. One season they lost only seven games on the road.

After winning their first pennant in 1949 the young Red Wings struggled past the Canadiens, led by Rocket Richard, in seven games in the first playoff round. Then they were wiped out by Toronto in four straight in the finals.

Ironically, the Wings won their first Stanley Cup while Howe was in the hospital recovering from his brush with death. After Howe was injured in the first game of the first playoff round, Detroit roared back in the second game and squared the series, by winning 3-1. Both Lindsay and Gus Mortson had fights with Leaf Ted Kennedy (who was involved in the play that injured Howe). One of the fights grew into a free-for-all. Toronto boss Conn Smythe conceded later, "The Lord and Twelve Apostles couldn't have kept the Wings under control tonight."

Tempers tamed after that. In Toronto the Leafs won the third game 2-0. The Wings again squared the series in the next game with a 2-1 victory. The winning goal was scored by Leo Reise in the ninth minute of overtime. He shot from the blue line and the puck ricocheted off several players before skimming past a startled Turk Broda in the Toronto goal. The series moved back to Detroit and the Maple Leafs won the sixth game 2-0 to take the advantage once again. The Red Wings were not discouraged, however. They tied the series at three games apiece as Lumley blanked the Leafs 4-0.

The seventh and deciding game was played in

Detroit. Tension slowly increased as the first and second periods went by without a score. At the end of regulation time, it was still 0-0. Lumley and Broda had both chalked up shutouts in regulation time.

Finally, in the ninth minute of extra play, Leo Reise ripped the disc past Broda for his second overtime goal of the series, sending the Red Wings on to the finals against New York.

The Rangers were in the finals for the first time in ten years. As had happened before, a circus in their home arena forced them to play all their games on the road. This time they played their "home" games in Toronto.

The Wings won the opener easily, 4-1, and may

Harry Lumley, the first in a string of great Red Wing goalies, stops a shot in the 1950 Stanley Cup playoffs.

have gotten overconfident. They lost the second game 3-1. Detroit won the third game, but New York won the next two, both on overtime goals by Don Raleigh. Once again the Wings were in the hole, trailing three games to two.

Early in the third period of the sixth game the Rangers had a 4-3 lead. They were only 19 minutes from winning the Cup when lethal Ted Lindsay sneaked inside and fired a shot past goalie Chuck Rayner to tie the contest. In overtime Sid Abel banged one home, giving the Wings a 5-4 victory.

The seventh game was a terrific tussle. Each side scored three goals in regulation time. In the closing minutes both made desperate attempts to score but were beaten back as the fans screamed themselves hoarse. There was no score in the first overtime period. Finally, in the ninth minute of the second overtime, Red Wing Pete Babando, who had scored only six goals all season but had already tallied seven in the playoffs, scored the biggest goal of his career, giving Detroit the game and the series. The jubilant Wings skated around the rink, holding the Stanley Cup aloft.

The 1951 Wings won a record 101 points and lost only 13 games during the regular season, but were beaten by Rocket Richard and Montreal in the first round of the playoffs. But they roared back in 1951–52 at full strength. Howe was at his best that year and Sawchuk was at the height of his powers. The Wings lost only 14 games all season, and stormed into the playoffs with confidence.

Detroit met Toronto in the first round. The Leafs tried everything including fists in the first game, as referee Bill Chadwick whistled a playoff record of 102 penalty minutes. Still, the Red Wings outskated and outscored the Leafs 3-0. Terry Sawchuk gained another shutout in the second game as the Wings won 1-0. They went on to sweep the series with 6-2 and 3-1 victories, leaving the Maple Leafs stunned and embarrassed. They headed for the finals against Montreal and Richard.

There are times when a talented goaltender gets hot and simply cannot be scored against. The final series was such a time for Terry Sawchuk. He swept away low shots with his stick and caught high shots with his glove. He moved with precision, leaping, diving, or doing whatever was necessary to stop the puck. He faced Richard's sizzlers without flinching and turned them all away. He gave up one goal in each of the first two games as Detroit won 3-1 and 2-1 at Montreal. He did not give up any goals in the last two games as Detroit won 3-0 and 3-0 at Detroit.

The amazing Red Wings had swept the playoffs in eight straight games (only the second time this had ever been done). Sawchuk had turned in four shutouts, the last two against Richard's Canadiens, in the greatest exhibition of goaltending in Stanley Cup history. He had given up a total of five goals in eight games. In the dressing room after the deciding game with Montreal, the sometimes sullen Sawchuk smiled and said, "Sometimes this is a beautiful life."

The Wings won their fifth straight pennant in 1953, but were surprised by Boston in the semi-finals and lost in six games.

In 1954, however, they won another pennant,

Heroes Terry Sawchuk and Sid Abel pose with the Cup after their 1952 victory.

then beat Toronto in five games in the first round of the playoffs.

So dynamic Detroit met mighty Montreal in the finals once again. The Wings took the first game 3-1, and lost the second by the same score. But the Canadiens were in trouble. Two of their stars, Doug Harvey and Jean Beliveau, were injured. The Wings won the next two games 5-2 and 2-0, taking a series lead of three games to one. The series seemed to be settled.

However, Canadien coach Dick Irvin turned to

his aging veteran goaltender Gerry McNeill, who
had been kept out of the earlier games of the series.
And in the fifth game he was magnificent. The two
teams battled scorelessly until the sixth minute of
overtime when Canadien Ken Mosdell backhanded
the black disc past Sawchuk for a 1-0 Montreal victory. In the sixth game the aroused Canadiens clobbered Detroit 4-1. So the series went to a seventh
game with the Canadiens trying to complete a
classic comeback and the Wings striving to save
themselves.

The game was a thriller. At the end of regulation
time the two keyed-up teams were tied 1-1. Then in
the fifth minute of overtime Detroit's Tony Leswick
lifted the puck high in the air toward the Montreal
goal. Defenseman Doug Harvey reached up to bat
the disc down, but it deflected off his glove, over the
shoulder of the Montreal goalie and into the nets.
The red goal light flashed and the Wings mobbed
Leswick in a joyous victory celebration.

The Canadiens, victimized by a freak goal, simply
left the ice, refusing to shake hands with the winning
Wings in the traditional post-game ceremony. In
their dressing room, Canadien coach Dick Irvin
said, "If I'd shaken their hands, I wouldn't have
meant it, and I refuse to be a hypocrite." He was a
bad loser, but his was an unlucky loss.

The Canadiens got their chance for revenge the
very next year. As the season neared an end in 1955,
Montreal led Detroit, threatening to end the Wings'
run of six consecutive pennants. But then Rocket
Richard was suspended by NHL president Clarence
Campbell for the rest of the season and the playoffs

Gordie Howe scores.

after Richard went on a rampage with his stick and his fists during a game.

In the very next game the Canadiens faced the Wings in Montreal. During the match fans assaulted Campbell, who was sitting in the crowd, and threw a tear-gas bomb on the ice. Campbell ruled that Montreal must forfeit the game to Detroit.

The Wings went on to win their last nine games and slip past Montreal by two points, winning their seventh consecutive flag.

In the opening round of the playoffs Detroit swept Toronto in four straight, by scores of 7-4, 2-1, 2-1 and 3-0.

Red Wing great Ted Lindsay lands on his nose during the 1955 playoff finals against Montreal.

In the finals Detroit faced Montreal for the third time in four years. Detroit broke up a close first game on Marty Pavelich's breakaway goal in the last three minutes and went on to a 4-2 victory. Then Ted Lindsay scored four goals as Detroit won 7-1.

At this point, another eight-game Stanley Cup sweep seemed to be in the making. But the Canadiens came back. In the third game Boom Boom Geoffrion scored three goals to carry the Canadiens to a 4-2 triumph. Then they scored a 5-3 win in the fourth game to deadlock the series.

In the fifth game Gordie Howe hammered home three goals to lead a 5-1 Red Wing romp and run his points for the playoffs to 19, a record. But, back in Montreal, the Canadiens battled back to win 6-3.

For the second year in a row, Detroit and Montreal faced each other in a seventh-game finals match. At Detroit's Olympia Stadium, with a capacity crowd cheering them on, Howe scored his ninth goal and 20th point, Delvecchio delivered two goals and Sawchuk stifled the Canadiens. The Wings won 3-1. The Canadiens had missed their chances for revenge and Detroit was still the leading power in hockey.

Since 1949 the Wings had won seven regular-season championships and four Stanley Cups. Gordie Howe had established himself as the greatest all-round player in the game and the other Detroit greats—Sawchuk, Lindsay, Kelly, Delvecchio— were close behind. But by 1956 the team was beginning to age. The young Montreal squad, led by young Jean Beliveau and veteran Rocket Richard, were already challenging Red Wing supremacy.

As Howe held the Stanley Cup aloft that April evening in 1955, skating triumphantly around the Olympia ice, he could not know that would be the last time in his incredible career. Detroit would reach the finals the following year and five times in the next 15 years, but the Red Wings would not again in that time sip champagne from the silver bowl.

7. The Greatest Team

In the early 1950s Montreal's Canadiens gave up Stanley Cup supremacy to the Detroit Red Wings. But the Canadiens were always dangerous, always a threat to the Red Wings, and they were building the base for a new team that would one day dominate hockey as no other team had ever dominated the sport.

Maurice "Rocket" Richard, that most spectacular of scorers, remained from the earlier championship Canadiens. But other stars were being added. Bernie "Boom Boom" Geoffrion, a powerful forward, fired in 50 goals one season, becoming the second man (after Richard) to accomplish the feat. Also up front were Dickie Moore, a clever sharpshooter; Bert Olmstead, an intense, unselfish playmaker; and the Rocket's kid brother, Henri Richard, a dazzling skater.

On the defense were Doug Harvey, a ten-time all-star, and tough Tom Johnson. In goal, Bill Durnan, the great goalie who had led the Canadien champions of the 1940s, had quit in the middle of a game in the 1950 playoffs and never played another game. "I couldn't eat. I couldn't sleep. I couldn't stand that sort of agony," he said.

Taking Durnan's place were Gerry McNeill, then Jacques Plante, the spidery acrobat who revolutionized his profession. Plante wandered all over the ice chasing loose pucks and perfected a mask to make tending goal a little safer. He won five straight Vezina Trophies.

The Canadiens showed their strength in the 1951 playoffs when they met pennant-winning Detroit in the first round. In the opener, the teams went into overtime tied 2-2. They fought through three scoreless extra periods. Rocket Richard broke up the game at 1:09 of the fourth overtime in the third longest game in hockey history, 121 minutes of playing time.

The second game also was tied at the end of regulation time, this time 0-0. And it stayed scoreless through two overtime periods. Finally, Richard, the classic clutch performer, stickhandled through the Wings, drew in the defense with a fake, then fired a fast shot past goalie Terry Sawchuk and into the nets at 2:20 of the third overtime.

Sparked by Richard and goalie McNeill, the Canadiens went on to upset the Wings in six games. Richard scored the tying goal in the 3-2 finale.

The Canadiens faced Toronto in the finals and every game went into overtime. The incredible Richard slammed in the 3-2 winner in the second game after two minutes of overtime. But Toronto swept the other four games and won the Cup.

Richard continued to astound everyone. He scored perhaps the greatest goal in Stanley Cup

Rocket Richard scores against Bruin goalie Jim Henry in playoff action.

playoff history in 1952. Montreal and Boston had three victories apiece in the opening round and were in the seventh and decisive game at Montreal.

In the second period, the roaring Rocket was knocked off balance by Leo LaBine. As he fell, his head slammed into the knee of defenseman Bill Quackenbush, then into the ice. He was unconscious and bleeding. Revived, he was helped to the dressing room. The gash in his forehead required six stitches and he was still very groggy, but he returned to the bench.

In the last period the score was tied 1-1. With four minutes left, Richard's linemate Elmer Lach saw Richard squinting at the clock and asked him what was wrong. The Rocket admitted his vision was blurred. Then he skated onto the ice with the rest of his line.

Near his own net, Richard took a pass from Butch Bouchard and started up ice. Carrying the puck on the end of his stick, he cut past one foe, veered to center ice and eluded another. Then he swept to the left and faked out a third Bruin as he angled toward the goal.

Both Boston defensemen, Quackenbush and Armstrong, moved toward him. They seemed to sense that the Rocket would not pass. Quackenbush skated into him, Richard whirled around in a complete circle, carrying the puck with him. Then he straight-armed the defenseman with his left arm, and bore to his right.

Bob Armstrong charged into him, but Richard restrained him with his left arm, shoving the puck ahead of him toward the goal with the stick held in his right hand. As goaltender Sugar Jim Henry dove for the puck, Richard one-handed it over and behind him into the net.

Single-handedly, he had beaten all six opponents, scoring the winning goal. The Montreal crowd came to its feet cheering and would not stop for five full minutes.

This story does not have a happy ending. In the Cup finals Detroit routed Montreal in four straight games.

The Canadiens recaptured the Cup the next season, 1953. This time they faced Boston, which had upset Detroit, in the finals. With Jacques Plante replacing McNeill in goal, Montreal won in five games. In a reversal of form, Elmer Lach scored the winning goal in the fifth game, assisted by Richard.

In 1954 and 1955 Detroit was back on top, taking both pennants and both playoffs in fierce seven-game struggles with Montreal.

When the 1955–56 season opened, however, the Canadiens had matured into a classic team. Toe Blake took over as coach and Richard, who had been suspended for the 1955 playoffs, was back, eager to revenge the two straight Cup losses to Detroit.

Richard was no longer the only big man on the team, however. Jean Beliveau had come to Montreal from amateur hockey as the most publicized and admired young player in many years. He lived up to his publicity. As unemotional as Richard was emotional, Beliveau was a strong, smooth player, as sure with a pass as with a shot. In 1955–56, his third full season in the majors, he scored 47 goals, leading the Canadiens to the pennant. The Canadiens won a record-setting 45 games, lost only 15 and tied 10 to become the first team to attain 100 points in a 70-game schedule. Then they captured the Stanley Cup in only ten games, defeating New York and Detroit in 5-game series. Beliveau scored twelve goals.

Four Canadiens—Beliveau, Richard, Harvey and

Detroit's Ted Lindsay has his shot blocked by the Canadiens' Jacques Plante in the 1956 playoffs.

Plante—were among the six men on the first all-star team. Johnson and Olmstead were on the second team. Beliveau was voted the Hart Trophy as the most valuable player, Harvey the Norris Trophy as the outstanding defenseman and Plante the Vezina

Trophy as the best goalie. Blake was voted Coach of the Year. This awesome team was selected in one poll of officials, players and writers as the best team in hockey history.

In 1957 the Canadiens were nosed out by the Red

During 1957 playoff action, Richard is foiled by the Bruin goalie.

Wings for the pennant. But the Canadiens were so powerful the league had to change a rule to keep them from gaining too great an advantage. Up until this time, when a player was serving a two-minute penalty, he had to serve out his full time no matter how many goals the other team scored. But with Geoffrion and Harvey playing at the "points" and Richard, Beliveau and Moore or Olmstead up front, Montreal's power play often scored two or three goals during a single two-minute penalty. According to the new rule the first goal scored by the opposing team automatically ended the penalty.

The Canadiens opened the 1957 playoffs against the New York Rangers. Montreal won three of the first four games. The fifth game went into overtime tied at 3-3. Then Rocket Richard rifled in an off-balance shot past Gump Worsley at one minute and 11 seconds of overtime to send Montreal into the finals.

Nearing 36 years of age, the Rocket gave one of his most remarkable performances in the opening game of the final round against Boston. The Bruins scored first against the Canadiens, but the Rocket tallied two straight in the second period to put the Canadiens in front. Then, after a goal by Geoffrion, Richard scored his third of the session.

In the last period, Henri Richard broke down the ice with his brother trailing him. Henri attracted the defenders, then dropped the puck behind him to Maurice, who drove in and fired a bullet which grazed the goaltender's arm on its way into the Bruin nets. It was the Rocket's fourth goal in the 5-1 game. The crowd of 15,000 Montreal fans gave the

Rocket one of the greatest ovations ever observed in sports.

The Bruins were broken. Beliveau's goal and Plante's goaltending gave Montreal the second game 1-0. Geoffrion's two goals helped Montreal to the third game 4-2. The Bruins stopped the Canadiens 2-0 in the fourth game, but Montreal scored a decisive 5-1 triumph in the fifth game to win the Cup for the second straight year. Boom Boom Geoffrion had scored eleven goals in the ten games.

Injuries hobbled the Canadiens the next season. Dickie Moore played the last five weeks of the season with a cast covering a fractured left wrist, but won the scoring title. Geoffrion missed the last part of the year with a ruptured bowel. The Rocket missed much of the season with a severed Achilles tendon.

But the Canadiens won the pennant and when they opened the playoffs in the Forum at Montreal against Detroit, Rocket Richard, back from his injury, scored two goals in the first four minutes. Montreal routed the Wings 8-1. Again, the Rocket tallied twice in the second game to lead his side to a 5-1 romp.

In the third game Andre Pronovost scored in the 12th minute of overtime to give the Canadiens their third straight win.

The fourth game of the series was Richard's 1,000th NHL game, and the incredible Rocket celebrated with style. With Montreal trailing 3-1 in the last two minutes, he scored three goals to win the game 4-3. Montreal had swept the strong Red Wings and qualified for the finals.

In the fifth game of the final series against Boston, with the series tied at two games apiece, the Rocket won another big one. At 5:45 of overtime he beat Boston 3-2. It was the 18th time he had scored a winning playoff goal. Said Richard, cracking a rare smile, "Scoring a winning goal in overtime makes you feel so young you can play forever."

The Canadiens captured the Cup for the third straight season in the sixth game as Geoffrion boomed home two goals in a 5-3 triumph. At the age of 36 Richard had scored 11 goals in the 10 playoff games.

In 1959 the Canadiens romped to another pennant. Beliveau scored 45 goals and Moore scored 41 and assisted on 55 for a record 96 points to win the scoring title. Richard missed the last three months with a broken ankle.

This year Montreal's playoff hero was the unlikely Marcel Bonin, who had never scored in 25 previous Stanley Cup games. In the first game, against Chicago, he borrowed a pair of gloves from Rocket Richard for "good luck" and promptly scored two goals and then hit for two more in the second game as the Canadiens won 4-2 and 5-1.

In the third game it appeared that Montreal faced disaster. Richard was already out of action. Now Beliveau was checked heavily by Glen Skov and suffered a serious back injury. The Black Hawks won 4-2. Bonin scored again in the fourth game, but Chicago's Bobby Hull scored his first Stanley Cup goal to get his team moving toward a 3-1 triumph. The series was tied at two games apiece.

Bonin scored again to help the Canadiens to a 4-2

After helping to win it for the third straight year, Rocket Richard poses with the Stanley Cup in 1958.

triumph in the fifth game. Then they took the sixth game and the series with a 5-4 triumph.

The champions moved confidently into the finals against Toronto. Bonin batted in the winning goal as the Canadiens won the opener 5-3. They won four out of five games, becoming the first team ever to win the Stanley Cup four years in a row.

In the dressing room after the last game, Blake said, "They say we're getting old, but we won this one without Beliveau most of the way and with

Richard very little of the way. They'll be back next season and so will we. I don't see why we can't win a fifth in a row."

There was no reason. This greatest of teams won its third consecutive pennant and fifth straight playoff in 1960. In the opening round of the playoffs, they played Chicago, winning in four straight.

In the finals against Toronto Henri Richard scored once and assisted three times in a 4-2 Montreal triumph in the opener. The Canadiens took the second game 2-1. Both Richards scored as the Cana-

The hero of the 1959 playoffs, Marcel Bonin, scores for Montreal against the Black Hawks.

diens won the third game 5-2. When the Rocket made his goal, he retrieved the puck from the nets to keep as a souvenir.

Montreal beat the Leafs 4-0 in the fourth game, completing an eight-game unbeaten march through the playoffs. With five straight Stanley Cup wins and three straight regular season championships, the Canadiens had reached the pinnacle of success.

The puck that Richard had taken from the nets was the last he ever whipped past a goalie. Before the next season he retired. Without him the team seemed to lack the spirit and inspiration in the short, intense playoffs. Montreal's mighty Canadiens won the pennant in 1961 and 1962. But they were upset in Stanley Cup play each season.

Still, the records had already been set. And when great teams of sports history are listed—baseball's New York Yankees, basketball's Boston Celtics—the Montreal teams of Richard, Beliveau, Geoffrion and Harvey must be right up at the top of the list.

8. Golden Jet in the Windy City

He took the puck near his own goal and circled behind the net with it. He started up the ice, using short, choppy strides that gradually lengthened out as he gathered speed. As he drove across the mid-ice line he lost one defender, who could not keep up. Another defender moved up to meet him at the blue line, but he faked to the right, then cut left without losing his tremendous speed. Now he was in the open, skates sending up a spray of ice as he went, thirty feet from the goal. He drew back his stick with a quick little move and drove it down and through the puck. The goalie could not help but flinch as the heavy, hard rubber disc came at his head in a blur. He stuck up his glove instinctively, but the puck ripped it off his hand and flew into the net. The red light flashed, signaling the goal. Bobby "The Golden Jet" Hull, raised his stick above his head of blond curls and the crowd cheered. The goalie scuffed his skates on the ice in despair.

Bobby Hull was only 22, and he was playing for the Chicago Black Hawks in the Stanley Cup playoffs of 1961. Some say this goal demoralized the

opposition, for Hull already was a frightening player. He was feared by goaltenders and defensemen alike. The chunky 5-foot-10, 195-pound Hull could carry the puck at close to 30 miles per hour, and one of his slapshots was later clocked at more than 118 miles per hour.

Hank Bassen, one of Detroit's two goaltenders that year, later admitted, "I've never been afraid of what I do [playing goal] or I couldn't do it. But when Bobby blasts one, he puts the fear of God in you. You see that thing coming at you like a bullet and your life flashes before your eyes. No one else ever shot so hard and so heavy. And if he hit a man with it, the man's skull could split open."

As it happened, the 1961 playoffs weren't Bobby's best, but they were important for the Chicago Black

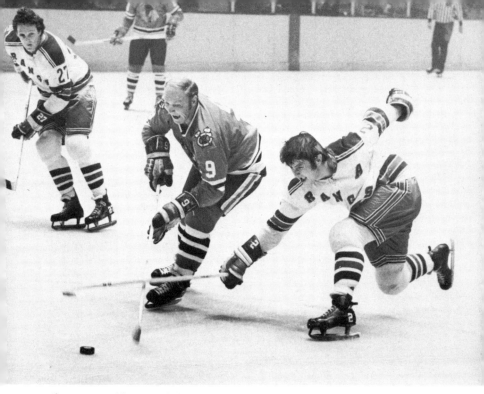

The great Bobby Hull fights for the puck with the Rangers' Brad Park.

Hawks. For 22 years the Hawks had sought the Stanley Cup without success. But with the Golden Jet to spearhead their attack and with superstar teammates Stan Mikita, Pierre Pilote, and goalie Glenn Hall, the Hawks finally took the Cup home to Chicago.

The story of the Hawks' long struggle for the Cup and their few successes begins with their first coach, Pete Muldoon. Muldoon was fired after his first season in 1927, and he supposedly predicted as he left, "Chicago will never enjoy the Stanley Cup." This prediction became known as "Muldoon's Curse."

In 1934 the Hawks won their first Cup and the curse was forgotten. Shortly after their victory the curse was remembered, however. They won the Cup, but because of a tragedy they were not able to enjoy it.

The Hawks had a great goaltender named Charlie Gardiner, the greatest in the game at that time. He was a happy-go-lucky fellow who was in his seventh season in the majors. Unlike many goalies, he didn't seem bothered by the pressures of his position. When the Hawks finished second, qualifying easily for the playoffs, Gardiner bet his teammate Roger Jenkins that the Hawks would capture the Cup. They agreed that the loser would push the winner in a wheelbarrow through Chicago's Loop (the main business district).

Gardiner was superb in post-season play. The first round was a two-game set with Montreal to be decided by total series goals. Chicago won the first game 3-2, and "lost" the second 1-0. But since this "loss" tied the teams in total goals, 3-3, the second game went into overtime. As in other sudden-death periods, the first team to score would win. Chicago's Mush March, who had scored only four goals all season, poked the puck past the Montreal goalie in the 12th minute of extra play to settle the series.

In the second round, in another total-goals pair, Chicago took on the other Montreal team, the Maroons. Gardiner blanked them in the first game, 3-0, and stood them off for a 3-2 decision in the second game. The Hawks had qualified for the best-of-five finals against Detroit.

The Hawks won the first two games of the finals in Detroit, 2-1 in overtime, and 4-1. In Chicago the Wings rallied to triumph 5-2 in the third game.

Major McLaughlin, owner of the Black Hawks, congratulates Mush March on his Cup-winning goal in 1934.

Then, in the fourth, Gardiner and his rival goalie Wilfie Cude dueled into a second period of overtime without allowing a goal. Then the low-scoring Mush March clipped the puck past Cude at 10:05 of the period for his second overtime winner of the playoffs.

Shutout hero Gardiner and the Hawks celebrated wildly. The next day Roger Jenkins wheeled Gardiner through the crowded streets of downtown Chicago in a wheelbarrow. Two months later Gardiner suddenly was stricken with a brain hemorrhage and died. Had Muldoon's Curse come true?

Four years later Chicago became the most unlikely holder of the Stanley Cup in hockey history.

The owner of the team, Major McLaughlin, knew little about the sport and operated the team as a toy. He wanted winners and had no idea how to get them. He hired and fired ten coaches in six years. One of them was a Hawk fan who met McLaughlin on a train and offered some ideas on running the team. Another was a baseball umpire and hockey referee, Bill Stewart. The Major figured a ref must know the game. Stewart was the coach in 1937–38 when the team won only 14 out of 48 games. They made the playoffs only because two of the eight teams had even worse records.

The only thing the Hawks had in their favor entering the playoffs was the curious playoff system of the time. In the first round the top teams of each division played each other. At the same time the two second-place teams and the two third-place teams played. In this way some top teams were eliminated well before the finals.

In the first round the Hawks upset the Canadiens in a three-game series and then surprisingly defeated the New York Americans. In both series Chicago lost the first game and came back to win the next two.

Suddenly the Hawks were in the finals against Toronto, which had upset the Boston Bruins in the first round. To add to Chicago's problems, the Hawks' goaltender, Mike Karakas, had broken a toe in the last game against the Americans. Just before the first game with Toronto, he discovered that the toe had swollen so badly, he could not get his boot on. He simply could not play. After a mad search for a substitute, the Hawks finally had to settle for a minor league goalie named Alfie Moore who had never played a game in the NHL. In a great substitute performance he made spectacular saves and the Hawks won 3-1.

Toronto manager Conn Smythe refused to let the Hawks use Alfie again in the second game. After another last-minute search, Chicago came up with Paul Goodman, who was supposed to be the substitute goalie in the first place. Goodman was no good this night and the Hawks were beaten 5-1.

By the time the teams got back to Chicago for the third game, Karakas' toe was improved enough so that he could put on his skate and play. He gallantly stopped the Leafs as the Hawks triumphed 2-1 on a goal batted in by Doc Romnes. The winning goal was hotly disputed by Toronto players, who said Romnes had been illegally in the crease and had illegally struck the puck with his hand.

A crowd of more than 17,000 turned out for the fourth game. Chicago was wild over their "wonder team," which had been lucky to even make the playoffs and now was within one victory of winning the Stanley Cup. Major McLaughlin was jumping up and down in his seat on every play and coach Stewart was screaming at his players in excitement.

Each team scored once in the first period. In the second period, Chicago's Carl Voss stole the puck from defensemen Jim Fowler and Reg Hamilton, skated in and rifled a ten-footer past the Leafs' goalie, Turk Broda, to put the Hawks back on top. A few moments later came a break which seemed to break the Leafs' hearts. On defense, Chicago's Jack Shill lifted the puck high in the air toward the To-

The Hawks lift manager Bill Stewart on their shoulders after winning the Cup in 1938. Mike Karakas is at bottom right.

ronto end 110 feet away. As it soared lazily toward the goal, Broda came out to make a routine stop of it, but he misjudged it. The puck bounced on the ice in front of him, hopped over his stick and rolled into the nets for a freak goal. The Hawks had a 3-1 lead and the fans came to their feet yelling.

The Leafs roused themselves to fight back in the final period, swarming all over the Hawks and sending a constant stream of shots at Karakas but they couldn't score. With four minutes left Doc Romnes of Chicago passed to little Mush March, the hero of the 1934 playoffs, who got a breakaway and beat goalie Turk Broda, to make it 4-1. That's the way the game ended.

The fans gave their heroes a standing ovation.

The Hawks rushed to Karakas, who was leaning against his cage, almost unable to move from the pain in his fractured toe, and they carried him off in triumph. Right behind them came little Mush March carrying the balding coach Stewart on his shoulders and staggering under the weight. In the dressing room, the Major was waiting to congratulate Stewart, who had won the world championship of hockey in his first try as a coach.

The next season the Hawks won only 12 games, finished last among all teams and didn't make the playoffs. Major McLaughlin fired coach Stewart.

Chicago still had never won a regular-season championship. After 1938 the next 20 years were a desert. Chicago reached the finals only once in all that time, and then they were swept out in four straight. Muldoon's Curse was remembered again. There was a stretch of 12 straight years in the 1940s and the 1950s when the Hawks finished last nine times and made the playoffs only once.

Things began to look up in 1956 when Tommy Ivan, the former coach of the champion Red Wings came in to rebuild the team. Pierre Pilote arrived in Chicago that year too. Pilote was a small but skilled playmaking defenseman who later won the Jim Norris Trophy as the best at his position three years in a row. Glenn Hall, an acrobatic goaltender who had played for Ivan at Detroit, arrived in 1958 along with Bobby Hull. Hall confessed he dreaded playing so much that he sometimes threw up in the dressing room before the game. Although he was always threatening to retire he was one of the great goalies in the sport.

Finally, in 1960 Stan Mikita arrived to round out the Hawk team. He was a small center, swift and agile on skates, good enough to get 30 to 40 goals a season, but even better at making great plays to assist on goals by others. He led the league in scoring points four times and two years in a row swept the scoring title, Hart Trophy as most valuable player and Lady Byng award for gentlemanly excellence.

Bobby Hull led the Chicago charge into the playoffs in 1961. The Hawks were a rough club trained by new coach Rudy Pilous to give a little extra. In the opener of the first-round series against Montreal, Chicago roughed up the Canadiens, but lost the opener 6-3. The Canadiens had won the Stanley Cup each of the last five years, so fans assumed that they would whip the Hawks. But Chicago came back to tie the series, winning 4-3.

In the third game, played in Chicago, the Hawks led 1-0 when Stan Mikita and Montreal's Bill Hicke got into a fight and were sent to the penalty box for two minutes each. They then got into a fight in the penalty box and referee Dalton MacArthur gave them additional five-minute major and ten-minute misconduct penalties. Since they both had nearly 17 minutes to sit out and the game was almost over, the ref sent them to their dressing rooms. They went and began to change into street clothes. Meanwhile, Chicago's Bill Hay drew a late penalty, shorthanding his team, and in the last minute, Henri Richard, ripped in the tying goal for Montreal, sending the game into overtime.

Before the overtime, Pilous told Mikita to put on his uniform again—he might yet be needed. And he was. Both teams narrowly missed shots in the first 20-minute extra period. One Montreal shot did go in, off the stick of Donnie Marshall, but referee MacArthur ruled he had hit the puck with the stick above shoulder level, which is illegal. MacArthur disallowed the goal, infuriating Montreal coach Toe Blake.

There were several narrow misses but no goals through the exciting second overtime and the two tired teams went to a third. A little past the midway point in the period, the Canadiens' Dickie Moore drew a penalty, leaving Montreal shorthanded. Chicago sent out its power play. Mikita got the puck on the point and tried a slap shot, but almost struck out on it. The puck dribbled toward the players camped in front of the Montreal net. Black Hawk Murray Balfour, standing with his back to the net, took the puck, whirled around, and backhanded it softly through Jacques Plante's legs and into the net. The Hawks had won the game and taken the lead in the series.

Montreal's run of five consecutive Stanley Cups was about to end. They came back to win the fourth game 5-2, but Hall blanked them by 3-0 scores in the fifth and sixth games. Montreal went home and the Hawks went into the finals against Detroit's Red Wings.

The teams alternated home games in the finals and the Hawks won the first one 3-2 on home ice. Then the teams alternated victories, each winning at home until the series was tied at two games apiece.

At Chicago in the fifth game the Hawks were leading 1-0 when they were hit by a penalty. Howe

Murray Balfour (top, far left) puts the puck into the net to win the third game against Montreal. At bottom, the Hawks' Glenn Hall makes a save against Detroit in the finals.

and Detroit were driving down-ice on a power-play when Chicago's Reggie Fleming stole the puck, broke away and scored a shorthanded goal. This goal seemed to turn the tide. Chicago went on to win 6-3, and two nights later they romped to a 5-1 victory to win their first Stanley Cup in 22 years. Winning a Stanley Cup was exciting to fans of the Canadiens—but in Chicago, the event was so rare that fans were nearly hysterical.

Still, maybe Muldoon's Curse was still in effect. The glow of winning the Cup was dimmed when Murray Balfour, who had won the wild third game with Montreal, died tragically of cancer at 29. And Rudy Pilous, who had become the coach when Tommy Ivan became general manager, was fired a few seasons later, even as Bill Stewart had been fired after 1939.

Billy Reay took over as coach and led the Hawks to their first pennant in 1967, but the Hawks lost the only other Stanley Cup final they reached in the 1960s and they were a luckless loser of one in 1971.

The year after Hull helped the Hawks to their Cup, he followed Richard and Geoffrion as the third player ever to score 50 goals in a single season. Then he became the first one ever to score more than 50 as he had seasons of 52, 54 and 58 goals. By the time he was a balding veteran of 14 seasons in the early 1970s, he had scored more than Rocket Richard's 544 and became the game's first $100,000-a-year performer.

What was Hull's greatest thrill? Winning the Most Valuable Player Trophy? Setting scoring records? Being voted the all-time all-star at left wing?

His wide, handsome face wrinkled into a smile and he said, "No, the big one was winning the Stanley Cup in 1961. A lot of great players never had a piece of it, you know. A lot of great players never had their name inscribed on it, and once it's there, it's there forever. That old silver thing, that's the real prize of this profession."

9. Punch's Senior Citizens

This was the sixth game of the 1962 Stanley Cup playoff finals. The Chicago Black Hawks, seeking their second straight championship, were down three games to two to the Toronto Maple Leafs. They needed this game to stay in the running. The contest was in the last period and there was no score. Then Bobby Hull, who had scored 50 goals during the regular season, shot a sizzler past Toronto goalie Don Simmons to put the home side in front. The Black Hawk fans went wild, throwing hats and coins and paper cups onto the ice. The game was delayed ten minutes while the rink was cleared.

The Hawks sensed victory, but Toronto was tough. Almost as soon as play resumed, the Leafs pressed in the Chicago zone and Leaf Bob Nevin bombed the puck past Chicago's goalie, Glenn Hall, to tie the crucial contest. The crowd was subdued for a moment, but the noise soon started again as the home fans rooted for their heroes to take the game.

It is tough to win on the road in any sport, but Toronto had a team of veterans who maintained their composure under pressure. One was Tim Horton, a superb skater who now took the puck in his own end and started up the ice. He passed it off, got it back, passed it off, got it back, and passed it finally to Dick Duff, who was streaking in on a wing. The play was perfect—Duff had a brief opening and he took it, shooting the puck into the net past Hall. Suddenly Toronto had a 2-1 lead. They held on and a few minutes later they had the victory and the Cup. Coach Punch Imlach clambered across the ice to lead the Leafs' celebration.

Toronto had gone ten long years without winning a Stanley Cup. In a town of great hockey tradition, Maple Leaf fans grew impatient, especially when

Punch Imlach smiles after a Toronto Cup victory.

arch-rival Montreal won the Cup five straight years from 1956 through 1960.

Punch Imlach had come to coach the Leafs in 1958, however, and in the next few years he began rebuilding. His method seemed strange—until Punch came along, poor teams were rebuilt by adding young players. But Punch, who was a veteran minor league manager and coach, rebuilt with veterans. He had some star youngsters, such as Frank Mahovlich and Dave Keon, but he kept the veterans he had and traded for more.

A fast-talking, hard-driving character, who had never been much of a player himself, Punch began collecting players like Red Kelly, Bert Olmstead, Bob Pulford, Andy Bathgate, George Armstrong, Mahovlich and Keon on offense. On defense he had Tim Horton, Carl Brewer, Allan Stanley, Bobby Baun and Marcel Pronovost. In goal he had Terry Sawchuk and Johnny Bower, two of the great goaltenders in history. Each of these players contributed to one or more Toronto teams which dominated the playoffs through the early 1960s. Many of them were in their 30s and some were approaching 40. Many were thought to be "washed up" by other teams that had traded them to Toronto. But Imlach seemed able to inspire them and make the most of their abilities. They won only one pennant in this period, but Imlach wasn't worried about that. He knew the real gold and glory lay in the playoffs and he simply nursed the Leafs through the season so they would be at their best when it counted the most.

Frank Mahovlich, a giant left-winger, came up in

1958, the same year as Punch. He was a brilliant player, scoring 48 goals in the 1961 season. But he was a worrier, a moody young man, who found it hard to live up to expectations that he would be another Richard, a Beliveau or a Hull. He was not a typical Imlach player and in later years he went on to star for Detroit and Montreal.

More typical was the skilled Red Kelly. He had been one of the great defensemen in hockey in Detroit. But the Wings thought he was past his prime and traded him to Toronto. Punch made him a playmaking center who gave this team inspiration. The intense Olmstead, cast off by the Canadiens, found he still had strong seasons left in his old legs. Goalie Johnny Bower was rejected by the Rangers after only one season in the majors and called "a minor leaguer." He came to Imlach's Leafs at the advanced age of 34 and lasted a dozen seasons, until he was 45. And temperamental Terry Sawchuk, another former Red Wing hero, came later to lend spectacular support for Bower in the nets.

In 1962 Toronto took on New York in the first round of the playoffs. Many of the Leafs were injured, but they kept playing. The Leafs won the first two games at home 4-2 and 2-1. But in New York, the Rangers won the next two, 5-4 and 4-2, to tie the series.

In the fifth game both Bower and Ranger goalie Gump Worsley were brilliant as the teams battled to a 2-2 tie at the end of regulation time. Then in the fifth minute of the second overtime, Kelly recovered the puck from Worsley, who had fallen to the ice, and fired it into the net to win the game for Toronto.

Maple Leaf goalie Johnny Bower goes after the puck.

Bower skated up ice to console Worsley, who shrugged and said, "We sure gave them their money's worth tonight." Gump had made 56 saves and he later admitted, "I was heartbroken." The fans gave him a standing ovation when he was introduced as one of the game's stars.

In the sixth game the Rangers collapsed and Toronto went into the finals against Chicago with a 7-1 triumph.

The Leafs won the first two games against the

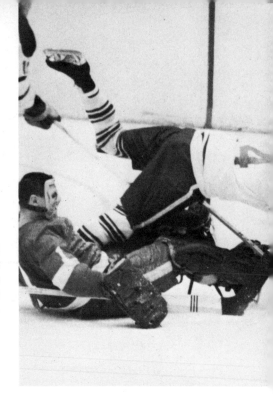

Toronto's Dave Keon (4) trips over Detroit goalie Terry Sawchuk, but the puck is in the goal in the 1963 playoff finals.

Hawks 4-1 and 3-2. But playing at home, the Hawks turned to tough tactics and Stan Mikita led them to a 3-0 triumph in the third game. In the fourth game Bower did "the splits" to reach a lethal Bobby Hull slapshot, but the force of it knocked him off balance and he pulled a muscle. Although he tried to continue, Don Simmons finally had to replace him for the rest of the series. The Hawks won 4-1.

In the fifth game Bob Pulford, playing with torn ligaments in his shoulder, scored a goal in the first 17 seconds and later banged in two more as the Leafs trounced the Hawks 8-4. This took the two teams back to Chicago for the sixth game. Veterans Nevin and Duff scored the winning goal as the Leafs came from behind to win 2-1, capturing the Cup for the first time since 1951. Back in Toronto thousands

cheered their heroes when they returned for a victory parade.

Some felt the 1962 win was a fluke, but Punch's Senior Citizens proved otherwise the following season. They nosed Chicago out for the pennant by one point and won the Cup again. In the first round, against Montreal, the Leafs won three straight, lost one and then won the deciding game on Bower's second shutout of the series.

Toronto met Detroit in the finals. In the first game Duff and Nevin scored two goals each and the Leafs won 4-2. They won the second game by the same score. The series moved to Detroit and Alex Faulkner scored the tying and winning goals in a 3-2 win for the Wings, but then Dave Keon paced the Leafs to a 4-2 triumph in the fourth game. In the sixth game before a home crowd, Dave Keon scored two goals, both when the Leafs were shorthanded, and the Leafs won 3-1. Toronto had its second Cup in a row. The aging athletes had surprised the sports world again.

And they were not finished. In 1964 they slipped to third place during the regular season and it appeared their reign was over, but they were fighters.

In the first round, against Montreal, they started poorly, losing to the Canadiens 2-0 on a shutout by Charlie Hodge. Montreal had been helped by the error of time-keeper George Ogg, who detained Dave Keon in the penalty box 33 seconds too long while Boom Boom Geoffrion scored the first goal. The fighting Leafs came back in the second game, however, as Kelly, Mahovlich and Bower tied the series with a 2-1 victory.

In Maple Leaf Gardens in the third game, Montreal's Henri Richard scored with just 25 seconds left to give Montreal a 3-2 nod. In the next game Toronto prevailed 5-3 to tie the series once again. But Toronto kept falling behind. They lost the fifth game 4-2. Now they needed to win two games in a row to qualify for the finals.

The never-say-die veterans were up to the challenge. Bower blanked the Canadiens 3-0 in the sixth game. Then in the seventh game their youngest player, Keon, scored three goals, and their oldest, Bower, frustrated the Montreal offense. Imlach's antiques won 3-1 to gain the finals against Detroit.

This was a tremendous series, which began with two games in Toronto. In the closing minutes of the first game the score was tied 2-2 and the Maple

Leafs were shorthanded. Then Bob Pulford electrified the crowd by driving the puck home with only two seconds left to win it for Toronto 3-2. The second game went into overtime and the Wings won in the eighth minute, 4-3.

The series moved to Detroit and the Wings won the third game when Alex Delvecchio scored with only 17 seconds remaining for a 4-3 verdict. The Leafs had fallen behind again, but Dave Keon tallied twice in the fourth game and Andy Bathgate scored the winning goal as the Leafs evened the series with a 4-2 triumph.

Bathgate had come to the Leafs late in the season. He was 32 years old and had been a pro for a decade without coming close to the Stanley Cup. One of the most spectacular and stylish performers of all time, he had played with the Rangers and had been a scoring champion, an all-star and even the league's Most Valuable Player without getting to play on a winner. Now he was within reach of his goal. He responded to his opportunity.

In the fifth game Gordie Howe drove in the winner for Detroit and Sawchuk stifled the Leafs. Detroit won 2-1 and took a lead in the series, three games to two. For the fifth time in the playoffs, Toronto had fallen behind. Again they would need two straight victories to win the series.

In the sixth game Toronto's body-checker Bobby Baun took a heavy blow and his ankle gave way under him. He collapsed in pain and was carried off on a stretcher. In the dressing room he insisted on being given a pain-killing injection so he could return to the ice. Meanwhile, the two teams were tied

Bobby Baun helped beat Detroit in the 1964 semifinals despite a broken bone in his foot.

3-3 as Bower robbed Detroit time and again of goals that would have given them the game and the Cup.

The contest went into overtime. In the second minute Bobby Baun, back on the ice, blasted a shot which deflected off Red Wing Bill Gadsby and into the net. Toronto had tied the series once again.

Like Andy Bathgate, Gadsby had never played on a Cup winner. He was 36 years old and had been one of the game's great defensemen for 18 years. Now he had landed on a contender and he spoke wistfully of winning his first Stanley Cup. Yet now he had become the "goat" in a crucial game. The Toronto hero, Bobby Baun, had scored only once in 47 previous Stanley Cup games. Now he had banked one in off Gadsby's leg to win the biggest game of his life. And he had done it on a broken ankle.

Incredibly, Baun insisted on getting another pain-killing shot so he could play in the seventh and deciding game in Toronto. The hungry Andy Bathgate put Toronto ahead 1-0. Goalie Bower held the fort during furious play until other Leafs found the range and put the game away 4-0. The Leafs had their third straight title.

It was Bathgate who held the Cup aloft as the Leafs skated triumphantly around the ice. Unlike Bathgate, the Wings' Bill Gadsby never played on a Stanley Cup winner.

The old Leafs faded out of the Stanley Cup picture for a couple of years after 1964. Some veterans, including Bathgate, did not appreciate Imlach's tough tactics and were traded. Punch made some changes, including a trade that brought him Terry Sawchuk to play when Bower needed a rest.

In 1967 the Leafs lost ten straight games during one stretch. Then Imlach collapsed and was hospitalized with exhaustion. While he was recovering, his assistant, King Clancy, brought the club out of its slump and when Punch returned, some players rebelled because they liked Clancy better.

But Punch was a tough man and a sharp operator. He took the team in hand and got them together by playoff time. They met the Black Hawks and Bobby Hull in the first round. Hull and Denis Dejordy were brilliant as the Hawks blasted the Leafs in the opener 5-2. In the second and third games the hero was goalie Terry Sawchuk, who had starred in playoff games before, but never for the Maple Leafs. Toronto won both games by 3-1 scores.

Ken Wharram, who played with Mikita on Chicago's "Scooter Line" of scrappy little players, scored after only nine seconds of the fourth game and the Hawks went on to win 4-3, tying the series. During the game Hawk goalie Glenn Hall, who still played without a mask, suffered a 25-stitch gash on his chin and lost two teeth when struck in the face by a shot from Jim Pappin.

In the fifth game Imlach started Johnny Bower in goal, but Bower was shaky. After one period, with the score tied 2-2, Terry Sawchuk, who had asked to be rested, came in for Bower.

Right away, Bobby Hull slammed the puck right at Terry. It glanced off his shoulder and struck him in the mask with such force that it knocked him flat. The trainer anxiously rushed onto the ice. He looked down at Sawchuk, who was still lying there, and asked if he was all right.

"I stopped it, didn't I?" Terry said. Then he got up and stopped everything Hull and the others threw at him for the rest of the game. The Leafs won the game 4-2 and went ahead in the series.

Toronto finished the series in the next game, winning 3-1. Brian Conacher, latest product of a famous hockey family, tallied twice and Toronto was in the finals against Montreal once again.

Could the old men pull it off once again? It seemed unlikely. The Canadiens had swept out the

Rangers in four straight games and had gone undefeated in 15 straight games. They seemed almost unstoppable.

A rookie, Rogatien Vachon, was playing goal spectacularly for the Canadiens down the stretch. But Imlach wasn't impressed. "You can tell that amateur goaltender that he won't be playing against a bunch of peashooters when he plays against the Leafs," he said.

When Vachon heard the comment, he said, "It was kind of Punch to mention me."

In the first game, played in Montreal, Henri Richard scored three times and Yvon Cournoyer twice as the Canadiens won 6-2. Sawchuk was troubled with injuries and seemed to be tiring fast, so Imlach started Bower in the second game. He shut out the Canadiens, 3-0, to end their undefeated streak and even the series.

Bower came back to face an unbelievable 60 shots in the third game. The Leafs battled into a second overtime before Bob Pulford, a hero in earlier Cup playoffs, fired the winning goal past Vachon.

In the fourth game Bower pulled a leg muscle in the pre-game warmups and Sawchuk had to limp back into action. He was blasted 6-2. But Terry came back determinedly in the fifth game and was beaten only once—on a deflected shot—as the Leafs won 4-1, to go ahead in the series three games to two.

Back in Toronto in the sixth game, Toronto took a 2-1 lead into the last minute of play. Montreal coach Blake pulled his goaltender and put six attackers on the ice in hopes of getting the tying goal.

Frank Mahovlich (27) and Ron Ellis (16) drive on the Montreal goal in the 1967 Stanley Cup finals.

Imlach went for experience, putting in some of his oldest, most experienced hands—Stanley, Horton, Kelly, Armstrong and Pulford. There was a face-off in the Toronto end. Stanley beat Montreal's Beliveau to the puck. He passed to Kelly, who passed to Pulford, who passed to Armstrong, who pushed the

puck into the empty Montreal net to sew up the 3-1 triumph. The Cup returned to Toronto once again and the fans in Maple Leaf Gardens stood and cheered their amazing old men.

In the dressing room a flushed and excited Imlach said, "This is the best one of all, the one that means the most because it was the one we were least expected to win. When we lost ten straight in the season and I was taken to the hospital, no one gave us a ghost of a chance, but we fooled everyone. We did it, and that beautiful cup is ours again." The television lights shone on his bald head as his aged athletes whooped and hollered like kids.

That was the end, however. The Leafs were too old to go any further. Some retired. Others were traded or sold. After the team slipped during the next season, Imlach was fired. The NHL had expanded and Imlach eventually took over the new team in Buffalo. The new team would take years of building before it would threaten for the Cup. But Punch had already set an enviable playoff record with the Leafs—and changed the game. He had proved that a player's prime may come late in life. After Punch's Senior Citizens, hockey stars would be encouraged to play for more seasons than ever before. In fact the star of the very next Stanley Cup playoffs was an aging veteran who had come out of retirement to play for a new team of old men, Glenn Hall of the St. Louis Blues.

10. Old and New

Although the Maple Leafs had won a surprise Stanley Cup in 1967, the dominant power in the NHL was still Montreal. The Canadiens had won the 1965 and 1966 playoffs and when the old Maple Leaf team folded after 1967, the Canadiens were expected to take the Cup "home" to Montreal once again.

But hockey fans were interested in other developments in 1967–68. The league had expanded, doubling in size from six to twelve teams. The established teams were grouped in an East Division, while the expansion clubs—Philadelphia, Pittsburgh, Los Angeles, Minnesota, St. Louis and Oakland—were placed in a West Division. The divisions would have their own pennant races, and play in the early rounds of the playoffs would be between division rivals. Then the winning team in each division would meet in the finals to play for the Stanley Cup.

To supply the new clubs with players, the league held a draft before the 1967–68 season. The established teams could protect their most valuable players, but the new clubs could choose from the

rest. Most of the players who went to the new teams were youngsters. But some of the best-known veterans went too. Glenn Hall went to St. Louis, Terry Sawchuk to Los Angeles, Andy Bathgate to Pittsburgh and Bob Baun to Oakland.

The new St. Louis Blues were run by Lynn Patrick, of the famous hockey family, and ambitious Scotty Bowman, a coach who followed the style of Punch Imlach. While the other new teams were starting up with youngsters, Bowman got such veterans as former Montreal stars Dickie Moore and Doug Harvey, and Al Arbour, Don McKenney and Jean-Guy Talbot. He also got one of the great goalies in hockey, Glenn Hall. During the season, Bowman also picked up a younger player, Red Berenson, who helped spark the team, but the Blues were basically an old squad.

St. Louis didn't set any records during the regular season. Philadelphia finished first in the new West Division with Los Angeles only a point behind. St Louis barely squeaked into third place, one point ahead of Minnesota's North Stars. But the Blues veterans were ready when playoff time rolled around.

St. Louis opened the playoffs against the pennant-winning Philadelphia Flyers. Goalie Hall immediately showed that he hadn't lost his touch, shutting out the Flyers 1-0. They went on to win three of the first four games, but the Flyers came back to tie the series at three games apiece. Then the Blues won the decider 3-1 in front of the amazing Hall.

In the semi-finals between St. Louis and Minnesota, the Blues lost two of the first three. The fourth

Ancient Glenn Hall stops a shot for the St. Louis Blues in the 1968 Cup finals. Hall was the goal-keeping hero for Chicago in 1961.

game stands as one of the classic contests in all Stanley Cup history.

Minnesota scored three times in the first two periods and led 3-0 midway in the third period. Then the Blues' Jim Roberts scored in the 12th minute of the period and Dickie Moore scored exactly one minute later. With only eleven seconds left, Roberts scored again to tie the game and send it into overtime. The St. Louis crowd was nearly hysterical. The Blues' Gary Sabourin scored in the second minute of overtime to win for St. Louis 4-3, tying the series at two games apiece. St. Louis had scored four goals in the last 10 minutes of play in a thrilling comeback.

The Blues won the fifth game in overtime but were slaughtered 5-1 in the sixth. This set up another crucial seventh game—another classic contest. Glenn Hall played superb goal for St. Louis but the Minnesota goalie was equally good. With only four minutes left the North Stars' Walt McKechnie scored the first goal of the game. It seemed that Minnesota would go on to the finals. But less than one minute later, old man Moore ripped the tying goal home for St. Louis, sending the game into overtime.

The first overtime was scoreless. In the third minute of the second overtime, Ron Schock of St. Louis slammed the puck home to end the exhausting series. St. Louis would be the first expansion team with a chance at the Stanley Cup.

Meanwhile, Montreal, the mightiest team in the sport, had nosed out New York for the regular-season pennant in the established East Division. In the first round of the playoffs they faced Boston and rookie superstar Bobby Orr. They demonstrated their power by blasting the Bruins, winning four straight games. If there was any doubt about Montreal's superiority, they dispelled it in the semi-final series against Chicago. Facing a great team, headed by Bobby Hull and Stan Mikita, they wrapped up the series in only five games. It seemed sure that the struggling St. Louis club would be outclassed and embarrassed by the Montreal powerhouse in the finals.

But Bowman's Blues were old pros who were not going to give up easily. They played the first two games at home and would have the support of cheering St. Louis fans. In the tenth minute of the first game, St. Louis defenseman Plager slammed in a shot to put the Blues ahead with the first goal of the series. Stung, Montreal struck right back as Henri Richard broke free and ripped in a shot 23 seconds later to tie the game.

Still, the Blues fought their established foes on even terms. Dickie Moore scored against his old team in the ninth minute of the second period to set St. Louis in front again. Late in the period, the Canadiens' Yvon Cournoyer, a blur on skates, whizzed one past Hall to tie the contest. Still, the Blues did not break. They battled through a scoreless third period to send the contest into overtime. In the second minute of overtime, however, Jacques Lemaire got the puck into the net to give Montreal a 3-2 victory.

The rematch two nights later was equally intense. It was scoreless for two periods. Serge Savard scored for Montreal in the third minute of the third period to put the Canadiens ahead. The Blues could not break through for a score, however. Their late bids were thwarted by old Gump Worsley in the Montreal nets and the Canadiens prevailed 1-0.

The series moved to Montreal's Forum. Most people expected that with the home-ice advantage the Canadiens would break the series wide open. But the Blues surprised them once again.

Late in the first period of the third game Frank St. Marseille scored, and the Blues took a 1-0 lead. Early in the second period the Canadiens were

Henri Richard tries to get the puck past the Blues' Glenn Hall.

shorthanded and the Blues were working the power play. Then Montreal's Serge Savard suddenly stole the puck, broke away and scored a shorthanded goal to tie the score. It was a costly goal for the Blues— they might have gone ahead 2-0 and instead they were tied 1-1.

Still, they did not surrender. Two minutes later Berenson bombed the puck past Worsley. The Canadiens came back to score again and the two teams went to the third period tied 2-2. After eleven minutes of play, Montreal's Ralph Backstrom ripped a shot home to put the Canadiens in front 3-2. But again the Blues refused to crack. With less than three minutes left Berenson scored his second goal to tie the game and send it into overtime.

All game, Montreal had dominated play and out-shot their foes by a wide margin, but they had been foiled repeatedly by Glenn Hall. But in the second minute of extra time Bobby Rousseau ripped one into the nets to give Montreal a 4-3 victory. The Blues had gotten only 15 shots compared to Montreal's 46, yet the Canadiens had needed overtime to win.

On a Saturday night in Montreal, Dick Duff scored late in the first period to give Montreal the first goal of the fourth game. The Blues were down three games to none and behind in the fourth game, yet they would not give up. Craig Cameron scored to tie the game in the seventh minute of the second period. Then one minute later, Gary Sabourin scored to put the Blues ahead 2-1.

St. Louis struggled to hold off the opposition's superior forces. But in the eighth minute of the last period, Henri Richard broke through for a goal to tie the game. Then J. C. Tremblay scooped the disc home past Hall to put Montreal ahead 3-2. In the final minutes, the Blues bore in trying to tie, but failed. At the final buzzer, it was 3-2 Montreal.

The Canadiens had won their third Stanley Cup in four years, winning twelve of thirteen games in the playoffs. But as the Stanley Cup was brought on ice to be presented to the Canadiens, the Montreal fans cheered the St. Louis Blues. St. Louis had lost four straight, but two were decided in overtime and all four were decided by only one goal. In some ways the Blues had performed better than Boston and Chicago against the Canadiens. They had struggled through two seven-game series to reach the finals. And they set a playoff record by engaging in ten overtime games, winning six. In many ways it was a classic series.

A member of the losing Blues, goalie Glenn Hall, was given the Conn Smythe Trophy as the outstanding individual performer in the playoffs. Old man Hall, who had helped win his first Stanley Cup twelve years earlier with Detroit, had kept things even between the Blues and the champion Canadiens. He was the series hero even though he worked in a losing cause.

After their victory over the Blues, the Canadiens suffered a blow when their coach, Toe Blake, announced his retirement. Since coming to Montreal in 1956, Blake had led the Canadiens to nine regular-season championships and won the Stanley Cup eight times.

A coaching change was not enough to upset the Canadiens' winning ways, however. In the 1969 Cup playoffs they overcame all opposition, again beating the Blues four games straight in the finals. But there was a cloud on the Montreal horizon—the great Boston Bruins. The 1969–70 season belonged to Bobby Orr and his teammates. In the meantime, Montreal did not qualify for the playoffs—for the first time in 22 years. The Bruins won the Stanley Cup, taking the finals from the hapless St. Louis Blues.

In 1971 the Bruins had been even better. Over the 78-game season, they had won 57 games (a record), lost only 14 and tied 7. They gained a record 121 points, finishing 12 ahead of New York, and 24 ahead of Montreal. It was the best season ever put together by an NHL team. Phil Esposito had set awesome all-time records with 76 goals, 76 assists and 152 scoring points. Meanwhile, Orr had set new records for defensemen with 37 goals, 102 assists and 139 points. He was voted Most Valuable Player for the second straight season.

Meanwhile, Montreal coach Claude Ruel had resigned in midseason and Al MacNeil had taken over. He had taken his team to a playoff spot, but the Canadiens were far down the list of possible Stanley Cup winners. Boston was the big favorite, and the Chicago Black Hawks and a strong New York Ranger team were close behind.

The Canadiens were a good offensive team. They had scored 299 goals, the third highest season mark in NHL history, but no one noticed because the Bruins had scored a record-shattering 399. The big

A new goaltender-hero for Montreal, young Ken Dryden, stops a shot by the Bruins' Ken Hodge in the 1971 playoffs.

Canadiens problem was defense and especially goal. Late in the season MacNeil had turned in desperation to a 23-year-old collegian, Ken Dryden. Everyone agreed that the 6-foot-4, 215-pound rookie was promising. But when the playoffs started he had only six games of major league experience.

The Canadiens had to open the playoffs against the favorites—the powerhouse Bruins. It was no surprise when Bobby Orr got the Bruins off to a fast start with a goal after four minutes of the opening

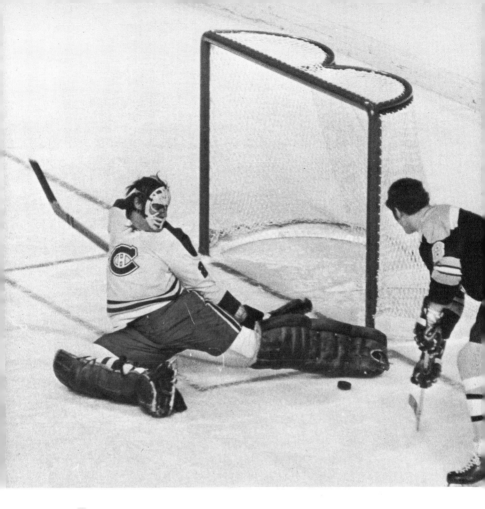

game, leading Boston to a 3-1 win. In the second contest the Bruins built a 5-1 lead and seemed to be running away from Montreal. But the Canadiens came roaring back, led by Jean Beliveau and John Ferguson. They won 7-5.

In the third game, the skillful Esposito whipped the puck into the nets before half a minute had gone by to put the Bruins on top 1-0. But then Ken Dryden rose to the occasion, shutting the Bruins out for the rest of the night. Meanwhile, big Frank Mahovlich, the former Toronto star now with Montreal, tallied twice and Montreal won 3-1, to take the series lead.

Mahovlich scored again early in the fourth game and Dryden protected the 1-0 margin to the midway mark. But the Bruins were growling. The incomparable Orr became the first defenseman in playoff history to score the three-goal hat trick, sparking a Boston rally for a 5-2 win.

With the series tied, the fifth game was played in Boston. Orr set up three goals, one by Esposito, and another by John Bucyk (who had scored 50 during the regular season). The Bruins drubbed Dryden and the Canadiens 7-3. The big Bruins were playing their kind of game again. Back in Montreal two nights later, however, Henri Richard and Peter Mahovlich scored twice each, and Montreal blasted Boston 8-3. Now the outcome of the series rested on the seventh game.

The crucial contest was played in Boston on a Sunday afternoon and was televised nationally. The Bruins' Ken Hodge scored first, early in the first period. But underdog Montreal fought back. Frank Mahovlich and Rejean Houle scored for the Canadiens before the period ended, and Montreal took a 2-1 lead.

Late in the second period Montreal's Gilles Tremblay got the puck past the Boston goalie and Montreal led 3-1. The mighty Bruins were on the ropes. At 14 seconds of the third period Frank Mahovlich slammed in another Montreal goal. Johnny Bucyk scored one for Boston, but Dryden turned back one desperate drive after another until the final buzzer. The Canadiens had won 4-2 and the favorite Bruins were eliminated.

Meanwhile, New York's Rangers had stopped Toronto in six games in the other Eastern preliminary. Over in the West, Chicago's Black Hawks, in their first year as a West Division club, swept out Philadelphia in four straight, while Minnesota ended St. Louis' string of three straight West Division playoff crowns, winning in six games.

According to the new playoff schedule, Montreal faced one of the West Division winners, Minnesota, while the Rangers played the Black Hawks. The Canadiens progressed to the finals, but needed six games to overcome the scrappy North Stars. The Black Hawks, meanwhile, squeaked by New York in a great seven-game series.

Pete Stemkowski of the Rangers won two games with overtime goals, but Bobby Hull finally made the difference, winning the fifth game in overtime and scoring the winning goal in the decisive seventh game.

So Chicago and Montreal met in the finals. The first two games were in Chicago. Montreal's Jacques Lemaire scored the first goal midway in the second period of the first game. But Bobby Hull evened the score early in the third period. They went into overtime. Finally, in the second minute of the second session, Jim Pappin knocked the puck past Dryden to give Chicago a 2-1 victory and the first win in the series. Dryden had been peppered with 58 shots. He gave ground in the second game, too, as Lou Angotti

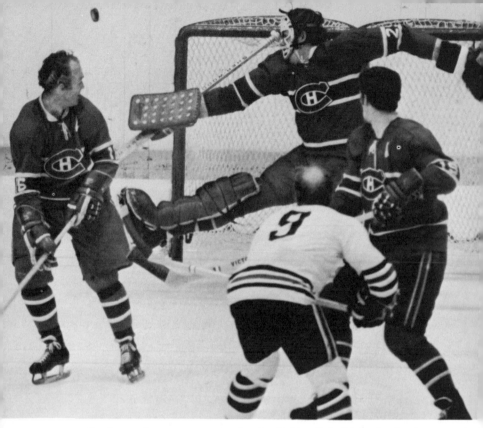

Dryden makes a save on a shot by Bobby Hull (9) in the finals.

tallied twice to pace the Hawks to a 5-3 triumph. Montreal was in trouble and fans began to wonder if Dryden could hold out.

In the third game Cliff Koroll and Bobby Hull scored to give Chicago a 2-0 lead. Down by two games and behind in the third, Montreal seemed doomed to defeat. But in the second period the brothers Mahovlich, first Pete, then Frank, scored to tie the contest. And in the third period Yvon Cournoyer and Frank Mahovlich scored to win it for Montreal 4-2. Dryden had stiffened again, shutting out the Hawks after their early scores.

Two nights later, Canadien Guy Lapointe pounded in a pair and Dryden held his ground. Montreal won, 5-2, to tie the series. But in the fifth game Chicago goalie Tony Esposito shut out the Canadiens as the Hawks won on goals by Dennis Hull and Cliff Koroll. The Hawks were within one game of their first Stanley Cup victory in ten years.

Worse yet for Montreal, there was dissension on the team. Veteran Henri Richard, disturbed because he had been left sitting on the bench, publicly called coach MacNeil "incompetent," and "the worst coach" he had ever played for. Richard was a major star and the brother of hockey's greatest hero. His graceless outburst made it almost certain that MacNeil would be fired after the playoffs, no matter who won the Cup.

The sixth game was in Montreal on a Sunday afternoon. Midway in the first period, Jim Pappin scored to put Chicago in front. But a minute later Yvon Cournoyer's goal evened the score. In the second period Pete Mahovlich put Montreal in front, but then Bobby Hull and Pappin shot Chicago back into the lead 3-2. In the sixth minute of the third period Frank Mahovlich tied the game with his 14th goal of the playoffs, a record. And in the ninth minute his brother Pete ripped one past Esposito to put Montreal on top 4-3. Dryden stopped the Hawks the rest of the way to save the victory for Montreal.

Now, Montreal had pulled even once again, but the final game would be played in Chicago. It seemed that the Hawks had the advantage at every turn. It had been the league's longest season. It was mid-May and summer-warm, and the players were tired. There were 21,000 eager Black Hawk fans in the ancient Chicago arena. Dennis Hull drove a shot past Dryden in the last minute of the first period, sending Chicago to a 1-0 lead. Kevin O'Shea beat Dryden in the eighth minute of the second period to make it 2-0 and it seemed all but settled. At the half-way point the Canadiens seemed doomed again. Had they come this far only to be beaten in the seventh game?

But then in the fifteenth minute of the second period Montreal's Jacques Lemaire lofted a high, long shot toward the Chicago nets. Somehow it escaped Esposito and slipped into the nets. It was a freakish shot, but the score seemed to give the Canadiens new life. With less than two minutes to play in the period Henri Richard, the malcontent, ripped the puck into the net to tie the game.

As the third period started, the fans were cheering on the Black Hawks. But then the amazing Richard, who had long played in the shadow of his brother the Rocket, got loose with the puck. Henri was 35 years old but he was still lethal. He cut loose and lashed in his second goal of the game to give Montreal a 3-2 lead.

Chicago did not give up. The Hawks put together attack after attack in a desperate effort to draw even. But Ken Dryden, immune to pressure, made stop after stop after stop. Finally the siren sounded, and it was all over. The underdog Canadiens, behind again and again, had won 3-2 and taken the

Montreal's Henri Richard drives in and shoots the puck past Hawk goalie Tony Esposito to win the Cup for the Canadiens.

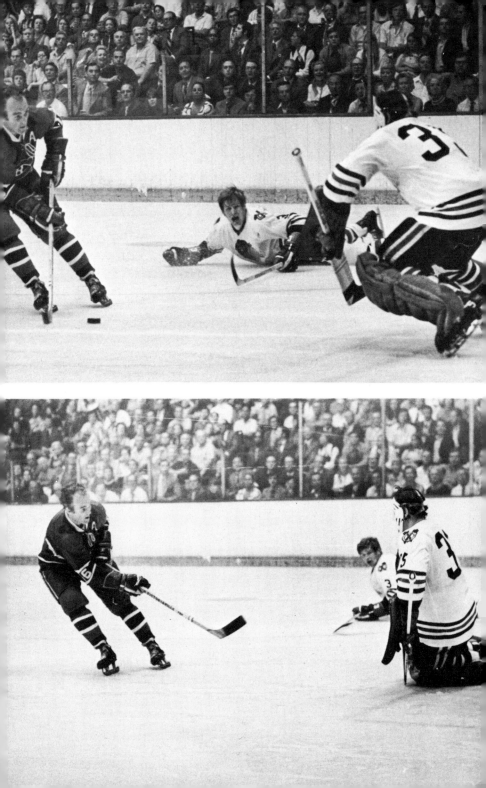

Stanley Cup once again. In the playoffs Dryden had played in all 20 games. He was voted most valuable player in the playoffs.

After the game he sat in the dressing room with sweat streaming down his handsome face. He smiled and confessed, "No, I wasn't nervous, I was just scared to death." Everyone in the Montreal dressing room laughed, even Richard. Coach MacNeil celebrated with the team, but he was soon fired for having lost control of his club.

In the Chicago dressing room, there was silence. The Hawks, Hull and Mikita and the rest, were not laughing.

Jean Beliveau, who had played his last season, posed with the Stanley Cup. In his career the Canadiens had won it eleven times. But the story of the 1968 and 1971 victories had been mostly the story of two goalies—old Glenn Hall, who had almost stopped the Canadiens single-handedly, and young Ken Dryden, who had stepped into the playoffs with only six NHL games behind him and sparked the most unlikely Canadien team ever to victory.

Canadien hero Jean Beliveau holds the Cup aloft after helping to win it for the last time. He retired before the next season.

Acknowledgments

The author wishes to thank all those who have written about the game and its history and so have contributed to this book. Special thanks is due to Ken McKenzie of *The Hockey News, Pictorial and World*, in whose publications so much of my work has appeared over the years. Also, thanks to Jack Kent Cooke, Larry Regan, John Wolf and others on the staff of the Los Angeles Kings, who graciously have provided me a base of operations in recent years.

Index